PAPERS ON FORMAL LINGUISTICS

No. 5

ADJECTIVES
AND
NOMINALIZATIONS

by

ZENO VENDLER

The University of Calgary

1968
MOUTON
THE HAGUE · PARIS

ACKNOWLEDGEMENTS

This work comprises revised versions of *Transformations and Discourse Analysis Papers*, 52 and 55 (Department of Linguistics, University of Pennsylvania). I prepared these papers while being a member of the National Science Foundation Project in Linguistic Transformations (University of Pennsylvania) during the academic years of 1959-60 and 1963-64. Throughout this time I greatly benefited by discussions with Z. S. Harris and H. Hiż. In addition to this continuous help I wish to express my gratitude to A. F. Brown, who first drew my attention to the order of prenominal adjectives and provided me with a large selection of actual examples, and to P. Ziff for his helpful criticism of my first results. In writing on nominalizations, I also profited by discussions with J. Munz, L. Gleitman, R. Koenigsberg, N. Sager and C. Smith. The work of B. Robbins (TDAP, No. 36-38 and 47, later published in an extended form in *Papers on Formal Linguistics*, No. 4, Mouton, The Hague, 1967) is presupposed in the first chapter of Part One. R. B. Lees' book, *The Grammar of English Nominalizations*, also helped me in preparing Part One.

Z. V.

CONTENTS

PART ONE

NOMINALIZATIONS

I. CONJUNCTIONS AND RELATIVE CLAUSES

1. Certain transformations unite two sentences into one. In the simplest case the ingredient sentences are merely joined by connecting particles like *and, or, because, since, therefore*, etc., without any further change; e.g.:

John is sleeping, but Mary is working
Mary will pass, because she works hard.

If the ingredient sentences share one or more elements, deletions may take place:

John is sleeping, but Mary is not
She went to high-school and then to college.

In the case of noun-sharing one sentence can be turned into a relative clause and inserted into the other sentence without any other connecting device:

Mary, who works hard, will pass
She goes to Oberlin, which is a good college.

The clause is formed by replacing the shared noun in one sentence by *wh...* (*which, who*, etc.) and inserting the result into the other sentence following the occurrence of the same noun there. Examples like

John, whom I saw yesterday, suddenly died

My car, the engine of which you ruined, is in the garage

show that the enclosed sentence often has to be rearranged so that the *wh...*, or the noun phrase containing the *wh...*, may begin the clause. There has to be, in other words, an apposition between the *wh...*, phrase and the corresponding noun in the enclosing sentence. For this reason, relative clauses of this kind are known as appositive relative clauses. It is not my purpose here to give detailed rules for the formation of such clauses or for the recovery of the ingredient sentences. I only note that in all these cases the structure of the ingredient sentences remains intact and the changes involve replacements, deletions and simple changes of succession only. Accordingly, by following simple rules, it is easy to recover the ingredient sentences, and these emerge from the analysis as complete sentences.

This also applies, in particular, to the *wh*...-replacement. The *wh*... replaces the noun as is, that is, together with its complement of articles, pronouns, quantifiers, adjectives, etc. This rule, however, does not imply that the segment replaced has to be identical with the corresponding segment in the enclosing sentence. While in

Mary, who works hard, will pass

He loves *his wife*, who is a good woman

Vipers, which are poisonous, should be exterminated

wh... replaces a segment identical with a segment (italicized) of the enclosing sentence, in cases like

(1) She loves a man, who lives in Paris

(2) He gave me three red apples, which were rotten

the *wh*... replaces a segment that cannot be found in the same form in the enclosing sentence. *Who* in (1), for instance, replaces *the man (she loves)*, and *which* in (2) replaces *the three red apples (he gave me)*. This fact, of course, indicates that the insertion of the appositive clause follows the completion of the enclosing sentence and does not enter into its formation. Consequently, in the process of decomposition we have to reproduce the enclosing sentence first and then reconstruct the enclosed sentence following the rules of sentence succession in a coherent discourse.

Thus we get for (1) and (2) respectively:

She loves a man. *The man (she loves)* lives in Paris.

He gave me three red apples. *The three red apples (he gave me)* were rotten.

The italicized segments in the second sentences are the ones that get replaced by the *wh*....

We can conclude, then, that it is necessary for the formation of an appositive clause that there exist in a discourse two sentences successive with respect to the same noun (or noun phrase). This noun, together with its complements, in the second sentence is replaced by *wh...* and the result (with eventual change in word-order) inserted into the first sentence.

As to decomposition, we first reproduce the enclosing sentence without the clause, then we reconstruct the enclosed sentence by replacing the *wh...* with the noun (or noun-phrase) to which it was attached and (after rearranging word-order if needed) add those complements to the noun in question that are necessary for the second sentence to be a continuation of the first in the same discourse with respect to the same noun.

2. The concept of succession in a discourse with respect to a noun will become clear as we proceed to consider the other type of relative clause, which is called restrictive relative clause.

Compare:

(3) Mary, who works hard, will pass
(4) Girls who work hard will pass.

The superficial difference is easy to describe. In (4), but not in (3), *who* can be replaced by *that*, and in (3), but not in (4), the clause is separated by pauses (commas in writing) from the enclosing part. This latter feature points toward a deeper difference: the clause in (4) is part of the subject noun-phrase of the enclosing sentence, while in (3) it is merely apposited to the subject-noun of the enclosing sentence. Indeed, while (3) easily splits into a conjunction of

Mary will pass

Mary works hard

(4) is more than a mere conjunction of

(5) Girls will pass
(6) Girls work hard.

The point of (4) is exactly the restriction of *girls* to hard-working ones. This means, of course, that (6) becomes incorporated into the subject of (5) by changing it to *girls who work hard.*

Certain noun-phrases are not open to such increment, simply because their denotation cannot be further restricted at all. I think of phrases like *Mary, my father, the man*, etc., i.e., those that are traditionally called *definite noun-phrases*. Indeed, we cannot get

*Mary that works hard will pass

*My father that is tall came in.[1]

Concerning *the man* and the like we have to realize that *the* itself is nothing but a sign of a restrictive clause present or deleted. Take

(7) The man (whom) you see wears a hat.

This is to be split into

(8) You see a man

(9) A man wears a hat.

One cannot argue that (9) should rather be

(10) The man wears a hat

because (10) is nothing but a contraction of (7):

The man [(whom) you see] wears a hat.

This can be shown by comparing the sequences:

(11) I see a man. The man wears a hat.

(12) I see a man. The man (whom) you see wears a hat.

We take (11) to be a continuous discourse: *the man* in the second sentence refers to the one I see. Not so in (12): *the man* there is the one you see, who may be different from the one I see. So (12) sounds discontinuous: I changed subjects. These facts can be explained by adopting the following hypothesis:

---

[1] There are exceptions to this restriction, like

The Boston my father knew is no more

The Napoleon of Elba was a bitter man.

See B. Robbins, TDAP No. 38, or *Papers on Formal Linguistics*, No. 4, 3.52. Yet I have reasons to think that it is not the proper name itself, but some deleted noun before it that carries the clause. Compare for instance,

My father knew a man. The man was a teacher.

My father knew Boston. *The Boston is no more.

The man in the first sequence is identified by a deleted clause (*whom my father knew*) formed from the previous sentence. Such a move is impossible in the second sequence: *the Boston* remains ungrammatical. This makes me think that *the Boston my father knew* comes from something like *the [aspect of] Boston my father knew*.

a) *the* is always the sign of a restrictive clause present or deleted;

b) if such a clause actually follows the noun, *the* belongs to that clause;

c) if no such clause follows, then *the* indicates a deleted clause to be reconstructed on the basis of an identifying occurrence of the same noun in an actual or presupposed previous sentence of the same discourse (about identifying occurrences in the sequel);

d) if no such occurrence is to be found, then *the* should be interpreted as generic *the* (which will be discussed later);

e) a noun once prefixed by *the* cannot receive any other restrictive clauses (in other words, it behaves like proper nouns, e.g., *John, Mary,* or other identifying phrases like *my father*).[2]

The in (12) depends upon the actual clause, (*whom*) *you see*, but *the* in (11) depends upon the deleted but recoverable clause, (*whom*) *I see*.

3.   As (4) indicates, restrictive clauses need not be identifying; in other words, there are cases in which the clause restricts the possible extension of the noun-phrase without achieving identification. The following examples may illustrate this point:

Snakes that are poisonous are dangerous

A snake that is poisonous is dangerous

The snake that is poisonous is dangerous.

These sentences are paraphrases of one another. Consequently *the* in the last sentence belongs to a clause that is non-identifying. Such an occurrence I call the generic *the*. Another example:

(13) Happy is the man whose heart is free.

Indeed, it would require poetic licence to continue (13) thus:

I met *him* yesterday.

The natural sequel is rather

I met *one* yesterday.

[2]   In certain special cases like *the Sun, the Hudson, the Pope, the Beatles* we can only guess the source; e.g.:

the river [(which is) called] Hudson

the group [(which is) called] Beatles

etc.

Now compare:

(14) The man that killed John wore a hat

(15) The man that asks shall receive.

The ingredient sentences of (14) are these:

(16) A man killed John

(17) A man wore a hat.

(16), then, is turned into the clause, *that killed John*, which gets inserted after *man* in (17). Since (16) is normally taken to be identifying, *the* is obligatory for *man* in (14). The analysis of (15) yields:

(18) A man asks

(19) A man shall receive.

Since (18) is not identifying, the relative clause obtained from it, *that asks*, does not make *the* obligatory in (15). So it will have the paraphrase

A man that asks shall receive.

Confusion might arise from the fact that in many cases it is not the clause but the enclosing sentence that is identifying; e.g.:

(20) A man who came from Albania killed John.

Now the clause *who came from Albania* is not necessarily identifying. This can be seen by considering generic sentences like

(21) A man who came from Albania has a lot to learn.

The enclosing sentence, however,

A man killed John

is identifying. So while it would be odd to continue (21) with

(22) The man wore a hat

such a sequel is quite natural to (20). *The man*, in that case, would be the remainder of *the man* (*that killed John*). It is also possible that the enclosed and the enclosing sentence jointly achieve identification. This, I think, is the case in the following context:

(23) Recently I talked to a man whom you introduced. The man said....

I should say that the deleted clause after *the man* in (23) is best reproduced as *whom you introduced and to whom I talked*.

It would require a long study to give the grounds on the basis of which a clause (or a set of clauses) can be or has to be interpreted

CONJUNCTIONS AND RELATIVE CLAUSES 17

as identifying. The presence or absence of tenses, modalities (like *should, would, must,* etc.) definite nouns (like *I, you, John,* etc.) are obviously relevant features. Yet no theory could draw a sharp distinction. There will be clauses that are clearly identifying, like the one in

He arrested the man that killed John.

There will be clauses that are clearly non-identifying, like the one in

Happy is the man whose heart is free.

But there will be a great many sentences that remain ambiguous in this respect. Take

(24) The man you love must be generous.

The original of the clause *whom you love,*

You love a man

may or may not be taken in an identifying sense. In the first case *the* in (24) is obligatory and (24) will have the paraphrase:

You love a man, who must be generous

where *who,* which introduces an appositive clause, replaces *the man you love* with an obligatory *the.* In the second case *the* in (24) is optional, so we get the paraphrases:

A man you love must be generous

Men you love must be generous.

The discovery that *the* can indicate a generic clause will not surprise us as we realize that even *he* or *she* can function in a generic sense. Indeed, (15) has the paraphrase

He who asks shall receive

where *he,* obviously, is a "generic" *he.*

4. As we shall see, restrictive clauses can be contracted by various deletions and other transformations. Thus it is clear that a sentence like

None but the brave deserves the fair

comes from

None but the [man who is] brave deserves the [woman who is] fair where both *the*'s are generic. Similar analysis is called for with respect to the sentences:

Only the expert can give an answer

This book is written for the mathematician

i.e.:

Only the [person who is an] expert can give an answer

This book is written for the [person who is a] mathematician.

Accordingly, there seem to exist the following patterns of contraction:

(25) the N wh... is A → the A

(26) the N_i wh... is an N_j → the N_j

where *the* is generic.

The second pattern enables us to account for the troublesome "short form" (i.e. without an explicit clause) of the generic *the*, which appears in sentences like

The tiger lives in caves.

It comes from

The [animal that is a] tiger lives in caves.

As the examples suggest, there has to be a genus-species relation between N_i and N_j in (26). In fact, if there is no such relation to be found (26) will not work. The sentence:

Objects are in space

does not have the paraphrase:

The object is in space

precisely because we do not find a suitable N_i to put into the slot in

The [—that is an] object is in space.

For similar reasons, while

The Incas did not use the wheel

is a paraphrase of

The Incas did not use wheels

the sentence:

The Neanderthal Man used the instrument

is not a paraphrase of

The Neanderthal Man used instruments.

In certain cases the generic *the* cannot be exchanged for the plural; e.g.:

Euclid described the parabola

i.e.:

Euclid described the [kind of curve that is a] parabola
or perhaps,

Euclid described the [class of curves that are] parabolas
is inadequately paraphrased in

Euclid described parabolas.

There are contexts that reveal the source of the "short form"
generic *the* more explicitly. Consider

(27) Only two kinds of large cat can be found in Paraguay:
the jaguar and the puma.

This gives away the source:

...the [(kind of) large cat that is a] jaguar and the [(kind of)
large cat that is a] puma.

And, notice, *the jaguar* or *the puma* cannot be exchanged in (27)
for *jaguars* or *pumas* nor for *a jaguar* or *a puma*.

Finally, not only N_i has to be the name of a proper genus in
(26), but N_j has to be the name of something like a "natural kind".
Thus while

The sabretoothed tiger was ferocious
passes all right, since the sabretoothed tiger is a kind of animal,
the generic sentence:

The dirty tiger is disgusting
is as odd as its origin:

The [(kind of) animal that is a] dirty tiger is disgusting.

To conclude this digression, the noun in the "short form"
generic phrase *the N* has to be the name of some species belonging
to a genus. To test whether a noun (or noun-phrase) N_j is sus-
ceptible to this form, we have to fit it into the schema:

the (kind of) N_i that is an N_j
which corresponds to the transform:

an N_j is a (kind of) N_i
If we find an N_i that is not trivial with respect to the given discourse, then the device works. But not otherwise. Thus *thing*,
entity, *being*, etc. will not do for discourses other than philosoph-

ical.[3] As a matter of curiosity, *man* does not fit into the schema;

    The man uses instruments

is not a paraphrase of

    Men use instruments.

Man, on the other hand, can have a generic occurrence without any article, as in

    Man, but not the ape, has language.

5.   Returning to the problem of the restrictive clause in general, we can summarize our results as follows:

    a) In order to generate a sentence containing a restrictive clause two ingredient sentences are necessary that share an indefinite noun.

    b) That noun gets replaced by *wh...* in the enclosed sentence and the result fitted into the enclosing sentence following the rules of rearrangement we mentioned in connection with appositive clauses.

    c) If the clause is taken to be identifying, then the noun to which it is attached has to obtain the definite article.

    d) The question, whether a given clause is or is not to be taken in the identifying sense, cannot be decided on grammatical considerations alone.

    e) A discourse is continuous with respect to a given noun, if those occurrences of the noun that are prefixed by *the* are followed by actual or deleted identifying clauses based on previous occurrences of the same noun in the same discourse.

    Thus we see that with respect to the article pertaining to the shared noun the situation is opposite between appositive and restrictive clauses. In the case of the former, the article in the enclosed sentence depends upon the enclosing sentence, while in the latter case the article in the enclosing sentence depends upon the enclosed sentence. To put it roughly, while the appositive clause follows upon the completion of the enclosing sentence, the restrictive clause precedes the completion of the enclosing sentence. This, of course, is in accordance with our earlier remark

---

[3]   In philosophical discourse, however, we may find sentences like

    The idea is more perfect that the object

    The object is in space, but the idea is not.

that a restrictive clause becomes part of the noun-phrase of the enclosing sentence, which is not the case in simple apposition.

6. The importance of understanding the genealogy of the restrictive clause increases as we realize that it marks one of the main paths along which a sentence can be incorporated into another. A great many transformations achieving this result can, in fact, be reduced to such clauses.

Here I do not mean trivial moves like the simple omission of the *wh...* as in

The man [whom] you see wears a hat

or the dropping of *wh... is* as in

The house [which is] on the hilltop is large.

Concerning these contractions I only remark that they seem to affect the restrictive *wh...* rather than the appositive one. Sentences like

*My father, you met, is a teacher

are deviant; others like

My new house, on the hill, is large

are more acceptable.

Some important transformations reducible to restrictive clause inclusions can be illustrated by the following examples (the shared noun is given in bold print and the enclosed sentence starred, once if not identifying, twice if identifying):

I see a yellow rose
I see a rose that is yellow

$\begin{cases} \textbf{A rose} \text{ is yellow*} \\ \text{I see } \textbf{a rose.}^4 \end{cases}$

He is a weak king

He is a king that $\begin{bmatrix} \text{rules} \\ \text{governs} \\ \text{etc.} \end{bmatrix}$ weakly[5]

---

[4] Concerning adjectival transformations see Part II for a detailed discussion.
[5] The idea of "appropriate" verb (or noun) classes, which is used here and in some of the following examples, is due to Z. S. Harris. Its importance can be appreciated as we compare *prima facie* intelligible adjectival compounds

⌈**A king** [rules, etc.] weakly*
⌊He is **a king.**

Such adjectival transformations conform to the rule given above according to which the shared noun must be an indefinite one, in particular, the rule that prohibits the reception of a restrictive clause for a noun prefixed by *the*. This rule accounts for the discontinuity in the discourse:

(28) I see a rose. The yellow rose is lovely.

Since the first sentence yields the identifying noun-phrase, *the rose I see*, the noun, *rose*, cannot receive another restrictive clause in a subsequent sentence that is continuous with respect to *rose*. So while

I see a rose. The rose is lovely.

is continuous, (28) is not. The following, however, is continuous again:

(29) I see a yellow rose. The yellow rose is lovely.

The analysis of the first half of (29) has been given above. In the second half the noun-phrase *a yellow rose* is shared by the ingredients as follows:

The yellow rose is lovely

The yellow rose that I see is lovely

⌈I see **a yellow rose****
⌊**A yellow rose** is lovely.

We can say, then, that in the order of generation a prenominal adjective can join a noun before but not after the reception of *the. The N* precludes additional adjectives much the same way as proper names do (think of **blond John, *fat Mary*, etc.).

Other moves that can be reduced to restrictive clause situations:

---

like *slow horse, good radio* with *prima facie* unintelligible ones like *slow chair, good planet*, or in case of compound nouns, as we compare the easily comprehensible *milkman, doghouse, nightshirt* with creations like *starman, milkshirt, nightman*, etc. It is obvious that the difference consists in the degree of availability of appropriate verbs permanently associated with the elements of the compounds. (See Part Two, VI, 2, pp. 88-94).

He is a milkman

He is a man that ⎡sells ⎤ milk
                ⎢delivers⎥
                ⎢handles⎥
                ⎣etc.   ⎦

⎰A man [sells, etc.] milk*
⎱He is **a man.**

Hardworking girls will pass
Girls that work hard will pass
⎰**Girls** work hard*
⎱**Girls** will pass.

He is a birdwatcher

He is a ⎡man ⎤ who watches birds
       ⎢boy   ⎥
       ⎢person⎥
       ⎣etc.   ⎦

⎰A [**man** etc.] watches birds*
⎱He is a [**man** etc.].

I met the writer of *Lolita*
I met the [man etc.] who wrote *Lolita*
⎰A [**man** etc.] wrote *Lolita***
⎱I met a [**man** etc.]

7. I add two corollaries of philosophical interest. First, it is obvious that in conjunctions formed by means of the appositive *wh*-clause, the ingredient sentences preserve their truth-value through the transformation. The sentence,

    She goes to Oberlin, which is a good college

is true if and only if the conjunction

    She goes to Oberlin and Oberlin is a good college

is true. In some cases, hoewever, the connecting particle should rather be *because, since, therefore,* etc. The following, for instance,

    Mary, who works hard, will pass

should be expanded into

>Mary will pass because she works hard

rather than into

>Mary will pass and she works hard.[6]

With respect to restrictive clauses, the situation is quite different. Identifying clauses indeed can be split into two subsequent sentences which are true if and only if the original is true. Take

>(30) I met the writer of *Lolita*.

This can be paraphrased as

>(31) A [man etc.] wrote *Lolita* and I met the [man etc.].

(31) brings out the "presupposition" of (30), i.e., that there is somebody who wrote *Lolita*. If the clause is not identifying, the truth relation becomes a conditional one.

>(32) Snakes that are poisonous are dangerous

is inadequately paraphrased as

>(33) Snakes are poisonous and snakes are dangerous.

While (32) is true, both parts of (33) are false. The conditional sentence, however:

>If a snake is poisonous then it is dangerous

is a true paraphrase of (32) or rather of

>A snake that is poisonous is dangerous.

The fact that (32) does not have the paraphrase (on the analogy of (31)):

>>Some snakes are poisonous and the ones that are poisonous
>>are dangerous

leads to the other corollary, which is this: while sentences containing identifying clauses do have "existential import", those containing non-identifying ones need not have. That is to say, while (30) can be paraphrased as

---

[6] It is interesting to notice that

>Mary, who will pass, works hard

is not paraphraseable by

>Mary will pass because she works hard.

The reason is that, as we said above, the source-sentence of the appositive clause has to occur later in the discourse than the enclosing sentence. If we resolve the original sentence in this sense, then *because* is ruled out, since

>Mary works hard because she will pass

is semantically objectionable. So we are left with

>Mary works hard and she will pass.

There is a man who wrote *Lolita* and whom I met

the sentence

Girls that have a perfect score get the prize

does not have the paraphrase

Some girls have a perfect score and they get the prize.

The conditional works again:

If a girl has a perfect score, she gets the prize.

II. PROPER NOMINALIZATIONS

1. As we have shown in detail, a restrictive clause incorporates a sentence into another by turning it into a part of a noun-phrase. It is interesting to realize that such incorporations nearly always occur *via* a noun-phrase. In other words, there are no standard and generally productive ways of transforming a sentence into a verb or adverbial phrase to be fitted into a host sentence. True, we have compound verbs like *birdwatch, babysit, gatecrash*, etc., which obviously come from some sentences, but their formation and decomposition fail to exhibit any general pattern and call for *ad hoc* moves. Consider:

He birdwatched for cranes

He gatecrashed the party

She babysat for Mrs. Walton.

No matter how we try, these sentences will not split into clear ingredients, and even if one finds possible candidates, the analysis will not work beyond the limits of the given example. It is very likely that these compound verbs are nothing but occasional re-verbalizations of certain agent-nominals, i.e. *birdwatcher, gate-crasher, babysitter*, which are indeed results of very productive transformational patterns. These, incidentally, can be reduced to restrictive clauses again:

birdwatcher — *N* that watches birds

gatecrasher — *N* that crashes a gate

babysitter   — *N* that sits with a baby

where *N* stands for a group of human nouns: *man, woman, person, boy, girl*, etc.

Again, one could argue that a sentence like

(1) He looked at the man through the window

comes from two original sentences

(2) He looked at the man

(3) He looked through the window.

These two being complete sentences, one might think that *through the window* is nothing but (3) incorporated into (2) as an adverbial phrase. But this is not so. For, while (1) has the (somewhat clumsy) transform:

His looking at the man was through the window

it certainly does not have the following:

*His looking through the window was at the man.

This shows that *through the window* in (1) is not a residue of (3) but an independent adverbial phrase, analogous to, say, *from the corner of his eyes* in

He looked at the man out of the corner of his eyes.

Here there is no parallel to the misleading (3);

*He looked out of the corner of his eyes.

is an incomplete sentence.

It appears, therefore, that the standard and universally productive ways of grafting a sentence into another amount to turning the sentence into a noun-phrase or part of a noun-phrase. I can only guess why this is so. If we consider the most common forms of elementary sentences, i.e.:

```
N V            N is A
N V N          N is N
N V N P N
etc.
```

we are struck by the versatility of nouns with respect to position. A noun can be the subject or the object of verbs, in the latter case direct or indirect. It can obtain prepositions, adjective- or noun-predicates, and it can become a predicate itself. By turning a sentence into a noun-phrase one gets a very adaptable result indeed.

However this may be, the fact remains that the incorporation of a sentence into another almost exclusively proceeds *via* a noun-phrase. Consequently, in a broad sense, all such operations could be called nominalizations. Yet in this paper my main concern will not be with nominalizations in this very wide sense. What I shall discuss in detail will be nominalizations in a narrower sense to be defined presently.

2. In all the examples of sentence incorporation hitherto mentioned we did, or we could, resort to the restrictive clause. This fact, of course, presupposes that the host sentence and the sentence to be grafted share a noun at the point of insertion. In the sequence *N wh...*, *N* belongs to the host sentence and *wh...* is a replacement of the same *N* belonging to the grafted sentence. Now this is not the case with what I shall call proper nominalizations. Some examples (the nominalized sentences italicized):

> I know *that he died*
> *His death* is unlikely
> *John's singing the Marseillaise* surprised me
> *His singing* was loud
> He shocked us by *telling a dirty joke*
> It is impossible *for him to succeed*
> *The selection of the jury* took up the afternoon
> *Helping the poor* is a duty
> I know *how to swim*
> *Life in China* is not easy
> He performed *the operation*
> It is better *to give* than *to receive*
> *The shaking of the earth* caused *the house to collapse*
> I watched *the criminal's execution*
> I saw *him die*
> I felt *the coldness of his hand*
> *His stupidity* is unbelievable
> *His presidency* began last year.

It is obvious that the sentences that appear in the list in a nominalized form do not share nouns with their host sentences, at least not at the point of insertion. Take, for instance,

(4) His death is unlikely.

The original of the nominalization, *his death*, is the sentence
(5) He dies.

The host sentence will be something like
(6) N is unlikely

but N here is certainly not identical with the only noun occurring
in (5), i.e. *he*. Therefore (4) cannot be reduced to the sentence
with a relative clause:
(7) *He who dies is unlikely.

The qualification added above, "at least not at the point of insertion", is necessary to avoid the impression that in the case of
proper nominalizations no noun-sharing can occur between the
host-sentence and the nominalized sentence. The example
(8) He shocked us by telling a dirty joke
comes from the sources
(9) He told a dirty joke
(10) He shocked us by N.

These share *he*. But the point at which the nominalization of
(9) gets inserted into (10) is not marked by *he* but by N. Consequently, in spite of the noun-sharing between (9) and (10), (8)
cannot be reduced to a sentence with a relative clause in it.

Then the question arises as to the nature of N in (6) and (10)
or, in general, as to the nature of the host-sentences that can
receive proper nominalizations. While, in most cases, the recon-
struction of the nominalized sentence is quite easy (think of (5)
or (9)), the host-sentence will remain incomplete, so that a symbol
(like N in (6) and (10)) or the dummy *it* has to be used to fill the
gap left behind by the removed nominalization. This fact affords
us a new look at proper nominalizations *versus* nominalizations
reducible to relative clauses. While sentences containing the latter
will yield two complete or almost complete sentences (missing
only *the* or some quantifier), the ones containing proper nominalizations will yield one sentence plus a sentence-root with a
noun-gap in it.[1] Moreover, as we are going to see in detail, this
gap will be a qualified one, inasmuch as in most cases it cannot

[1] Harris speaks of "one and a half" kernel forms.

be filled by original nouns, but only by nominalized sentences, and, depending upon the sentence root that contains the gap, only by nominalizations of a certain sort. The gaps, for instance, in the sentence roots:

...is unlikely

He shocked us by...

cannot be satisfied by putting in *John, stone, lion, table,* etc. Similarly the gaps in

...is a duty

...takes place at noon

He performs...

...is unlikely

...causes...

require proper nominalizations of some kind or other. Some such gaps, however, are not quite pure, inasmuch as they are suited for both nominalizations and genuine nouns. The roots:

I saw...

I know...

can take proper nominalizations, as in

I saw him die

I know that he died

and common nouns, as in

I saw the table

I know Paris.

3. It appears, then, that proper nominalizations represent a new and clearly definable way of incorporating a sentence into another, which is quite distinct from the one operating through the restrictive clause.

In order to facilitate subsequent discussion I shall stipulate the following terminology:

the noun-phrase resulting from a proper nominalization I shall call *nominal;*

the sentence undergoing such a nominalization I shall call *matrix;*

the sentence-root with a noun-grap suited for a nominal I shall call *container;*

the compound resulting from the fitting of a nominal into an appropriate container I shall call *nominal compound.*

Illustration: the nominal compound

His death is unlikely

fits the nominal

his death

which comes from the matrix

He dies

into the container

...is unlikely.

Then we can say that a proper nominalization is a transformation that turns a matrix into a nominal to be received by an appropriate container. The rest of this part will be concerned with a detailed description of the grammatical forms nominals can take, of the kinds of containers, and of the co-occurrence restrictions between forms of nominals and types of containers. As an indirect result we will obtain the grammatical background for the conceptual distinctions between objects on the one hand and facts, events, processes, actions, etc., on the other.

To summarize the content of these two chapters, we have distinguished three different ways in which two sentences can be merged into one. The first way is mere conjunction effected by connectives or the appositive *wh....* This way does not involve any essential change in the structure of the ingredient sentences. The other two, the one operating through the restrictive clause and the other through the proper nominalization, amount to incorporating a sentence into another *via* a noun-phrase. In the restrictive clause situation one sentence becomes a complement to a shared noun in the other sentence. In the case of proper nominalizations, one sentence becomes a noun-phrase to be fitted into a noun-gap the other sentence, or rather sentence-root, originally contains.

III. COMPLETE NOMINALS

1. The ease with which the list of nominal compounds given in the previous chapter could be continued indicates that speakers of the language have a clear intuition about proper nominalizations. It can be shown, moreover, that this intuition is not based upon some superficial and easily discernible grammatical feature that would mark all nominals. True, most nominals contain a verb-root, usually with a characteristic suffix like *-ing, -ion, -ment*, etc., but this condition is neither necessary nor sufficient. We feel that the following sentences that contain noun-phrases satisfying this criterion would not belong to the list:

This is a racing car

I eat John's cooking

My father is a judge.

The reason is obvious. Although all these sentences contain a noun-phrase with a verb-root in it, the operation that yields these phrases is not the proper nominalization but the restrictive clause insertion. The sources are:

...car that is [suitable] for racing

...[food] that is cooked by John

...[man] that judges [people]

or something similar. Accordingly, the host-sentences are not real containers. Indeed, we can substitute the noun-phrases in question by genuine nouns without spoiling grammaticality; e.g.:

This is a car

I eat John's food

My father is a tall man.

On the other hand, there are sentences that clearly belong to the list of nominal compounds, yet the nominals they contain do not have verb-roots at all. Remember the last three items on the list:

I felt *the coldness of his hand*

His stupidity is unbelievable

His presidency began last year.

Noun-substitutions in these cases yield questionable or somewhat elliptical results:

I felt his hand

John is unbelievable

?The man began last year.

Other nominals, however, can easily be substituted; e.g.:

I felt the shaking of the earth

His having won the race is unbelievable

The fight began last year.

We have to conclude, therefore, that the intuition we mentioned above goes deeper than superficial grammatical features; it corresponds, in fact, to the structural concept we developed in the previous chapter. Yet the grammatical shape of nominals cannot be ignored. We mentioned in the previous chapter that containers are selective with respect to the kind of nominal they are able to receive. It is quite easy to find convincing examples illustrating this point. Take the containers (with the noun-gap indicated as "○"):

(1)   ○ surprised me

(2)   ○ occurred at noon

then try the nominals.

(3)   his death

(4)   that he died

(5)   his having died.

Clearly (1) can take (3), (4) or (5); (2) can take only (3). Again the containers:

(6)   ○ is slow

(7)   ○ is unlikely

discriminate among the nominals:

(8) John's singing the Marseillaise

(9) that John sings the Marseillaise

(10) John's singing of the Marseillaise.

(6) can take only (10), but (7) is receptive to (8) and (9) but hardly to (10). The difficulty increases as we realize that the sequences:

John's death

John's arrival

are understood in different senses according to the quality of the container. While the sentences:

John's death surprised me

John's arrival is unlikely

have the paraphrastic transforms:

That John died surprised me

That John arrives is unlikely

the sentences:

John's death was slow

John's arrival is noisy

do not have the transforms:

*That John died was slow

*That John arrives is noisy.

Consequently, an adequate treatment of nominalizations will have to include the description of the various kinds of nominals, their transformational relations, and the co-occurrence restrictions between families of nominals and families of containers. We are going to find that these tasks are inseparably bound together.

In order to make a beginning, I shall try to enumerate first all the possible forms in which nominals can appear and to find some purely grammatical and transformational relations between them. In this task, provisionally, I shall ignore the various types of container in which these nominals appear, although, as I just suggested, the completion of this task will not be possible without them. Of course, the mere fact that the forms I am going to discuss will be of nominals indicates, according to the very concept of proper nominalization, that they are to be received by containers of some sort or other.

The method I am going to follow will be this: I shall start with nominals that distort the matrix least and proceed towards those that distort the matrix most. It is obvious that a nominal like

(11) that John has arrived

contains the matrix in a less distorted form than the nominal in the compound:

(12) Life in China is not easy.

(11), in fact, contains the matrix:

John has arrived

intact, only *that* is added. The matrix, on the other hand, from which *life in China*, in (12), comes, clearly underwent some fairly radical changes.

2. Consequently the least distorted nominal will be the *that*-clause:

(a) NV+ → that NV+[1]

We might add, however, that a sentence even without *that* can be regarded as if it were nominalized. Consider the examples:

He died, which surprised me

John has arrived. This was the result of clever planning. *Which* and *this* indicate noun-phrases here, which just are not there. For this reason, purists object to this move. One might say that the word *fact*, or something like it, has been deleted after *which* or *this*, but even then the difficulty remains: that John died or that he arrived may be facts, but we do not have *that* in the examples. We have to say, therefore, that in these and similar contexts the sentence concerned is presumed to be nominalized by virtue of an apposited noun or pronoun. This move may be called nominalization by proxy. At any rate, all such cases can be transformed into the *that*-clause.

---

[1] $V+$ represents the verb followed by whatever object it has; e.g.:
    (John) wins the race
    ("   ) puts the book on the table
etc. $V-$ will mark verbs not followed by their object; e.g.:
    (John is hard to) please
    (I know what he) ate.

As to (a), it is clear that it succeeds in turning a sentence into a noun-phrase. This we realize as we try to fit the result into the noun-slots of elementary sentence-types (I gave a list in the previous chapter). n indicates the nominal. Thus we get:

nV+   That he died surprised me
N V n   I know that he died
n is A   That he died is unlikely
n is N   That he died is a fact.

We fail, however, with *Pn*, as in *NVNPn*:
     *She based her hopes upon that he died.
In this case we have to involve an apposited noun:
     She based her hopes upon the fact that he died
or use a transform
     She based her hopes upon his death.
This is the first indication that the product of (a) is not quite a perfect noun. There will be others.

3. The next nominal to be considered also keeps the matrix intact, but adds *whether*:

n V+   Whether he died puzzled me
NV n   I wonder whether he died
n is A   Whether he died is uncertain
n is N   Whether he died is a mystery.

Pn fails here too. Thus we have:

     (b) NV+ → whether NV+

The difference between *that* and *whether* is not merely semantic. The "problematic" flavor of *whether* versus the "assertoric" flavor of *that* is reinforced by the fact that it is possible to add *or not* to the result of (b). This can occur two ways:
     whether or not he died
     whether he died or not.
The semantic difference can be indicated by the type of containers (a) and (b) tolerate; e.g.:

I think that he died

*I wonder that he died

*I think whether he died

I wonder whether he died.

But about this later.

Two additional remarks. *That* may be dropped in NV**n** compounds:

I know he died

I expect he'll come.

In the same NV**n** position *whether* can yield to *if*:

I wonder if he came.

One might think that *that* and *whether* nominalize a matrix through a deleted noun like *fact* or *question*. Indeed, in some cases we can insert these nouns without harm; e.g.:

I know the fact that he died

The question whether he died puzzled me.

The point is, however, that in many other contexts this move cannot be made:

*I think the fact that he died

*Tell me the question whether he died.

Such a difference may be relevant to the nature of the respective containers, but for our present purposes it is enough to say that (a) and (b) are nominalizing transformations on their own, without a deleted *fact* or *question*.

4.   The next class of only slightly distorted nominals are similar, but only superficially, to the products of (a) and (b). These are introduced by a group of *wh*...'s: *who, which, what, where, when, why, how.* Some examples:

I wonder who killed the grocer

What he found is uncertain

Where he can be puzzles me

Why he did it is a secret

How he got there cannot be explained

I don't know when he'll come

and so forth. The source of these nominals is fairly clear: some

element of the matrix, subject, object or adverbial phrase is replaced by the appropriate *wh....* The difference, therefore, from
(a) and (b) is that while there the nominal contains all the elements
of a complete matrix, here the nominal contains a substitute for
a noun or adverbial phrase of the matrix. Consequently, when
retracing the transformation, the matrix will emerge incomplete,
so that another substitute (*something, someone, somebody, some-
where, sometime, somehow*, etc.) has to be employed to obtain
a complete sentence. We can represent this form of nominalization as follows:

(c) S (some...) → n (wh...)

Spelled out in detail:

some... V+	→	wh... V+
NV some...	→	wh... NV−
NV+ sometime	→	when NV+
NV+ somewhere	→	where NV+
NV+ somehow	→	how NV+
NV+ for some reason	→	why NV+

The result of (c), by and large, is similar to a relative clause. The
main morphological difference seems to be that while *which* is the
most common *wh...* marking a relative clause, it cannot occur
by itself in (c):
    *I wonder which burned down.
It can occur only in connection with another noun:
    I wonder which house burned down.
What, on the other hand, clearly fits (c). The fact that *what*
also occurs in relative clause situations (amounting to *that which*
or *the thing which*) causes an interesting ambiguity. Compare
what he lost in
    (13) I know what he lost
    (14) I found what he lost.
Now add:
    (15) It was a watch.
Then (14) and (15) jointly entail that it was a watch that I found.

(13) and (15), however, do not entail that it is a watch that I know. What I know is that it was a watch he lost, but what I found is the watch he lost. Similarly, while

What he lost is a watch

is a transform of

It is a watch that he lost

the sentence:

What he lost is a mystery

is not a transform of

It is a mystery that he lost.

Fortunately, other *wh...*'s do not lend themselves to this confusion. Sentences like

*He arrested who killed the grocer

?I visited where he lives

are substandard.

The similarity between the relative clause and the standard product of (c) indicates the economy of language. The same, or nearly the same, morphological change produces a result that can be used in two totally different ways. And, as we know, the same change is used again as the first step in question-transformations concerning noun or adverbial phrases as in

Who did it?

How did he get the money?

etc.

5.   The discrimination of the next two classes of nominalizations, which I shall call (d) and (e), is a matter of extreme difficulty. The language seems to be undergoing a change at this point, so that the distinctions suggested by morphological differences are often overruled by co-occurrence tolerance and transformational behavior. Consequently, in this chapter I can only start the task of clarification, the completion of which will be left to a subsequent chapter dealing with containers. Since the most characteristtc feature of both (d) and (e) is the suffix obtained by the verb-root from the matrix, I start this discussion with a survey of the relevant suffixes.

The most common suffix is *-ing*. All verbs, except some aux-iliaries like *shall, can, may*, are able to receive *-ing: running, building, winning, being, having*, etc. In addition to *-ing* we have a group of other suffixes, which, for reasons to be given soon, I shall call "strong" suffixes, versus the *-ing*, which can be either strong or weak. The main varieties of the strong suffixes are as follows:

zero:	*run, walk, study*, etc.;
-ion:	*explanation, motion, division*, etc.;
-ment:	*movement, ailment, involvement*, etc.;
-al:	*refusal, disposal, reversal*, etc.;
-ure:	*mixture, departure, rupture*, etc.;
-th:	*death, birth, growth*, etc.;
others:	*life, thought, laughter*, etc.

Some verbs can have more than one strong derivative: *disposal, disposition; move, motion, movement*; etc. In some cases the (usually Latin) verb has no English equivalent: *fraction, fracture, lecture, conjecture*, etc. In case the matrix has *be A* or *be N*, not *be* but *A* or *N* obtains a strong suffix. Some of these suffixes of "abstraction" are illustrated in the following examples: *manhood, directorship, presidency*, etc., for nouns, and *redness, brutality, likelihood*, etc., for adjectives.

At this point I have to warn once more against a possible con-fusion. Not all the occurrences of these suffixes indicate proper nominals; often they occur in noun-phrases that can be reduced to relative clauses. Thus, *running* in, say, *the running water*, is an adjective. The zero-suffixed *judge* and *cook* are "agent" nom-inalizations and so can be *explanation*. Others may occur as "object" or "product" nominalizations, like *cooking, painting, creation*, etc. Some examples:

The explanation can be found on page seven

I eat John's cooking

I sold a painting.

Now it is clear that the host-sentences are not real containers, and the noun-phrases in question can be reduced to the relative clause:

> [The text] that explains [the phenomenon] can be found on page seven
>
> I eat [food] that is cooked by John
>
> I sold [something] that was painted by [somebody]

or something similar. Fortunately, other suffixes marking agent or object nominalizations do not occur in real nominals, so that confusion does not arise. Thus *runner, speaker, actor, investor, detergent*, etc., clearly denote agents, while *divorcee, addressee,* etc., denote objects.

The reason for discriminating between strong and weak suffixes can be given as follows. Let us call the unchanged verb-object and adverbs verb-complements and the restrictive clause and its derivatives, like the definite article and prenominal adjectives, noun-complements. Then we can say that V_{ing} can take either an unmixed set of verb-complements or an unmixed set of noun-complements; the product of V and a strong suffix, which I shall represent as V_n, can only take an unmixed set of noun-complements. This shows that the effect of a strong suffix on the verb is more radical than that of the weak suffix. While the former, metaphorically speaking, kills the verb as a verb and turns it into a noun, the latter may leave the verb alive.

Some examples of V_{ing} with verb-complements:

> winning the race
>
> comparing Mary with John
>
> putting his feet on the table
>
> running fast
>
> deliberately not answering the question
>
> having won the race
>
> being utterly stupid.

It is clear that V_n's do not tolerate verb-complements:

> *refusal the gift
>
> *painfully death
>
> *comparison Mary with John
>
> *utterly stupidity

V_n's, however, take noun-complements:

> the refusal of the gift
> the slow movement
> his utter stupidity.

But so can V_{ing}'s:

> the running of the race
> his continuous singing of arias.

Yet not even V_{ing}'s tolerate mixed packages:

> *his slow singing the Marseillaise
> *the winning the race
> *the suddenly breaking of the window
> *the slowly walking.

6.   Now we are able to define (d) and (e), at least in their pure forms. (d) splits away the subject of the matrix by adding the suffix *'s*, and then adds *-ing* to the verb, which keeps its verb-like complements; e.g.:

> (d) NV+ $\rightarrow$ N's Ving +

Some examples:

n V+	John's having won the race surprised me
NV n	He admitted John's being able to win
n is A	His winning the race is unlikely
n is N	His having won the race is a fact
NVP n	He talked about John's having won the race.

The result of (d) suggests a genitive structure comparable to

> (16) John's house.

But this analogy is misleading. While (16) has the transform:

> (17) the house of John

a result of (d), like

> (18) John's winning the race

cannot be transformed into

> (19) *the winning the race of John.

As we said above, V_{ing}+ cannot tolerate noun-like complements that come through the restrictive clause. *The* in (17), however. marks a restrictive clause in the source:

> the house [which belongs to] John.

Therefore (19) is impossible. So we have to say that *John's* in (16) and *John's* in (18) are different. Only the former is subject to the transformation:

(20) N_i's N_j — N_j of N_i

There is another difference, too. In any N_i's N_j that is subject to (20) N_i's can be dropped as follows:

John's hat is old. → The hat is old

I see John's house. → I see the house

etc. This is not true of N's in (d):

John's winning the race is unlikely

His singing aloud shocked me

do not go into

*(The) winning the race is unlikely

*(The) singing aloud shocked me.

We have to conclude, then, that (d) operates *in indivisibili:* $V_{ing}+$, by itself, is not a noun-phrase, so N's $V_{ing}+$ is not a proper genitive structure; it is one noun-phrase, not two.

As to verb-like complements, $V_{ing}+$ can take them without limit; e.g.:

His putting his leg on the table in front of the president shocked the company

His being able to learn French correctly in half a year cannot be expected

etc. What (d) has to leave out are modalities and imperfect past tense, owing to the limitations of the *-ing* suffix. Fortunately, as some of our examples show, the past tense can be expressed by using *have*, and *can* may be supplemented by *be able to*. Because of this limitation, we might have to add tense or a modal auxiliary when recovering the matrix.

For instance, for

I expect his coming tomorrow

His coming yesterday surprised me

the matrices will be

He will come tomorrow

He came yesterday.

The N's $V_{ing}+$ is subject to negation: N's $V_{ing} + \rightarrow N$'s *not* $V_{ing} +$; e.g.:

> his not arriving on time
>
> his not having won.

And to the passive: N_i's V_{ing} $N_j \rightarrow N_j$'s *being* V_{en} *by* N_i; e.g.:

> his being beaten by John.

Above we saw that the subject noun cannot be dropped from N's $V_{ing}+$. This impossibility is remedied in the passive, in which *by N* is a mere adjunct. Thus, we can say:

> His having been beaten is a fact.

It is worth noticing that matrices containing *be A* or *be N* are also subject to (d):

> His being stupid is unlikely
>
> His being the president worries me.

Here we must beware of the temptation to equate *his being stupid* with *his stupidity*, or *his being the president* with *his presidency*. We mentioned that the latter forms have strong suffixes, so they cannot tolerate verb-like complements. *N's being A* or *N's being N* require verb-like complements but refuse noun-like ones. The following examples show this clearly:

> *his long being the president
>
> *the being stupid of John
>
> *his utterly stupidity.

Containers and transforms show the same thing:

> (21)   His stupidity is incurable
>
>   *His being stupid is incurable
>
> (22)   His presidency lasted for three years
>
>   *His being the president lasted for three years.

True, *his stupidity* or *his presidency* can occur in containers suited for (d)-nominals too, as in:

> His stupidity surprised me
>
> His presidency worries me

but then these have the transforms:

> That he is stupid surprised me
>
> That he is the president worries me.

(21) and (22), on the other hand, are not transformable as follows:

*That he is stupid is incurable

*That he was the president lasted for three years.

As we shall see, this situation is by no means a unique one. We will encounter many cases in which morphologically "strong" nominals occur in "weak" containers. But this is the main difficulty we have to face later on.

The last move, that is, offering a product of (a) as a paraphrase for a product of (d), is of capital importance. Let us represent the product of (a) a, the product of (b) b, etc. Then we have the paraphrastic transformation:

(α) $d \Rightarrow a$

I call this a paraphrase in the following narrow sense: For all values of d, the corresponding a will satisfy all the containers d satisfies. Let Ct_d stand for containers that can receive d's and let d_i and a_i represent products of (d) and (a) from the same matrix. Then (α) indicates that the following will be a transformation for all values of Ct_d and d_i:

$$Ct_d \ [d_i] \ + \ \rightarrow \ Ct_d \ [a_i]$$

While (α) is a paraphrase, the following is not

$a \Rightarrow d$

Counterexample:

I think that John won the race

does not go into

*I think John's winning the race.

Yet even (α) has a flaw: it fails in ...P n containers:

I counted on his winning the race

*I counted on that he would win the race

He talked about John's coming tomorrow

*He talked about that John will come tomorrow.

But this is a negligible shortcoming. It merely shows that d is more noun-like than a.

7. Now e is still more noun-like than d. For e nominalizes the matrix by affixing a strong suffix to the verb-root, or by affixing

-ing with complements and morphological changes which are typical
of nouns. The result is a genuine noun-phrase, which then
can enter into a real genitive structure with the subject of the
matrix. This move, therefore, requires, among others, the following
transformations (V_n now will indicate verbs with a strong suffix
or the "strong" *-ing*, i.e. the one that carries noun-like complements):

(23) $NV \rightarrow N$'s V_n
(24) $NVD_A \rightarrow N$'s A V_n^2
(25) $N_iVN_j \rightarrow N_i$'s V_n of N_j

Examples with containers:

n V+	John's speech lasted for an hour
NV n	I watched her beautiful dance
n is A	His singing of the Marseillaise was loud
n is N	His death was a slow process
NVP n	I listened to his long speech.

Since, as I said, *N's* in (23)-(25) is a real genitive, it is subject
to (20). This is obviously so in case of (23) and (24):

(26) N's $V_n \rightarrow t\ V_n$ of N
(27) N's A $V_n \rightarrow t\ A\ V_n$ of N

where *t* is usually *the*, but not necessarily so; e.g.:

A speech of John's lasted for five hours
I heard a firing of the gun.

The result of (25) usually refuses (20). Yet, in some cases, it
can be forced into the mold:

That singing of arias of his kept me awake all night.

Since we are dealing here with a real genitive structure consisting of two noun-phrases, the subject-noun can be dropped
in every case. Thus, the products of (26) and (27) are subject to
the deletions:

(28) $t\ V_n$ of N $\rightarrow t\ V_n$
(29) $t\ A\ V_n$ of N $\rightarrow t\ A\ V_n$

[2] D_A here denotes an adverb (like *slowly*), while *A* stands for the corresponding adjective (*slow*).

Even (25) has an analogous result regardless of the missing intermediate step:

(30) N_i's V_n of $N_j \rightarrow t\ V_n$ of N_j

Examples for (28)-(30):

The speech lasted for an hour

The loud singing kept me awake

I heard the singing of the Marseillaise.

Since the products of (26) and (30) look alike, phrases like

(31) the shooting of the prisoners

will be ambiguous. If this is a product of (26), then the matrix is

The prisoners shoot

if it is a product of (30), then it is

(Somebody) shoots the prisoners.

The confusion increases as we realize that even the "objective genitive" in the product of (30) has a "backlash" transformation:

(32) $t\ V_n$ of $N_j \rightarrow N_j$'s V_n

which produces a form similar to the "subjective genitive" in (23). Thus even

(33) the prisoners' shooting

will be ambiguous. Here, in fact, we have a triple ambiguity, since this phrase, owing to the absence of complements, can be a pure d too. But about this later.

The reason why I call N_j's V_n in (32) a "backlash form" is the following. In the first place, while both (31) and (33) are ambiguous, the following is not:

(34) the soldiers' shooting of the prisoners.

Thus, if both nouns are present, *of N* is the "natural" form of the objective genitive and *N's* is the "natural" form of the subjective genitive. One might think that the lack of ambiguity in (34) is merely due to the similarity of sequence between the matrix:

$N_i\ V\ N_j$

and the nominal:

N_i's V_n of N_j.

But this is not so. It can be shown that the so-called subjective and objective genitives are morphologically different.

This is clear in the case of personal pronouns and proper names. Consider first:

(35) his shooting

(36) the shooting of him

(37) the shooting of his.

Obviously, in (37) he is the one that shoots, in (36) he gets shot and in (35) he can be either. This shows, that in all *e*'s, *of* followed by the accusative of *N* marks the objective genitive, but *of* followed by the genitive of *N* marks the subjective genitive. In case of personal pronouns, the latter requires "possessive pronouns", *mine*, *yours*, *hers*, etc., which are distinct from the "possessive adjectives", *my*, *your*, *her*, etc. Proper names do not have an accusative suffix, but they have a genitive one: *'s*. Thus while

Mary's shooting

the shooting of Mary

are ambiguous,

the shooting of Mary's

is not. Incidentally, the situation is similar in the noted triad:

(38) my picture

(39) the picture of me

(40) the picture of mine.

Here the ambiguity concerns possession *versus* representation. (40) is clearly a case of possession, (39) is that of representation and (38) may be either.

Consequently, at least in theory, the confusion of subjective and objective genitive disappears, as we correct the relevant transformations in the following manner:

(25a) N_i V N_j → N_i's V_n of (acc) N_j

(26a) N's V_n → t V_n of (gen) N

(27a) N's A V_n → t A V_n of (gen) N

(28a) t V_n of (gen) N → t V_n

(29a) t A V_n of (gen) N → t A V_n

(30a) N_i's V_n of (acc) N_j → t V_n of (acc) N_j

(32a) t V_n of (acc) N_j → N_j's V_n

If the verb, unlike *shoot*, is necessarily transitive, then the *N's V_n*

and $t\ V_n\ of\ N$ forms are rarely ambiguous. Even in the semantically loaded examples

the arrest of the sheriff

the hangman's execution

the feeding of the mother

the guard's capture

the overturning of the man

the genitive is an objective one. Of course, one can read ambiguity
into some examples, but it requires some effort:

The president's appointment took place yesterday.

Note, that the nominal in

The Senate approved of the President's appointment

is a pseudo-*e*, which, as we shall see later, is paraphraseable by
the corresponding *d*:

The Senate approved of (somebody's) being appointed by
the President.

Consequently, it appears that the product of (25a) is structured
as follows:

(25b) N_i's $\big[[V_n]\ of\ (acc)N_j\big]$

whence first $N_i's$ and only then *of* (*acc*) N_j can be dropped. Rep-
resenting necessarily transitive verbs by V^o, we get the unchange-
able sequence of deletions:

(41) N_i's V_n^o of (acc) $N_j \rightarrow t\ V_n^o$ of (acc) $N_j \rightarrow t\ V_n^o$

This excludes

? t V_n^o of (gen) N_i

? N_i's V_n^o

Indeed

*The lighting of the man

*The fireman's extinction

do not exist in spite of the fact that men light matches and firemen
extinguish fires.

(25a) takes care of the *e*-nominalization of matrices with a
direct object. What happens if the verb-phrase is not just VN

but *VNN*, *VPN*, *VNPN*, *VPPN*, etc.? Well, it seems that the technique is not yet adopted for such complexities. For most of the examples we can come up with are more or less questionable:

> ? his patient putting up with his wife
> ? our unanimous election of him president
> ? his putting of his leg on the table
> ? the comparison of Mary with Jane.

PN adjuncts fare better:

> the plane's slow flight over the city.

As I remarked above, *N's* in *d* is different from the subjective *N's* in *e*. The latter is a true genitive, the former is not. This comes out beautifully in the comparison:

> (42)   He shocked us by telling a dirty joke
> (43)   *He entertained us by singing of arias.

His is deleted after *by* in both compounds. This does not spoil (42) but ruins (43). The reason is that since (42) contains a *d*, *his* is not a real genitive, but remains the subject of a sentence. Consequently it is sufficiently similar to the *he* in the container; (43), however, contains an *e*, so *his* is a true genitive. Thus it is not similar enough to the *he* in the container to be dropped.

A little reflections shows that abstract forms such as

> his short but eventful presidency
> his long and incurable illness

are products of (e), for *N is N* and *N is A*. I represent the relevant transformations as follows:

> (44) N_i is $N_j \rightarrow N_i$'s $N_{j\ hood}$
> (45)   N is A $\rightarrow$ N's A_{ness}

As we see, the purely morphological discrimination of *d* and *e* forms is a difficult but not impossible matter. True, there are ambivalent forms; e.g., *N's* V_{ing} without complements can be a *d* or an *e*, provided *V* is not necessarily transitive. Thus

> John's singing

is a *d* in

> I mentioned John's singing

but an *e* in

I imitated John's singing.

Think of (α), which works only in the first case.

The real difficulty, however, is due to the fact that most e-forms can occur in d-containers, and in that case they can be paraphrased by the corresponding d-forms or even, through (α), by the corresponding a-forms. This tolerance is one-sided: morphologically clear d-forms cannot occur in e-containers. This latter restriction is clear from many examples I quoted, and I add a few here:

*I listen to his singing arias

*John's singing aloud lasted for an hour

*His singing the Marseillaise was out of tune

*His dying painfully was a slow process.

On the contrary, d-containers are tolerant indeed:

I mentioned his sudden departure

contains a strong suffix with a prenominal adjective;

The functioning of the engine surprised me

contains a subjective genitive;

The prisoner's execution is unlikely

contains a strong suffix with an objective genitive;

The declaration of the war is a fact

contains the same. Yet the containers are d-containers; for one thing, the a-paraphrase works in all cases.

The tendency to use the strong nominal, e, instead of the weak one, d, is so strong that some d's sound clumsy or even questionable in the same containers:

I mentioned his suddenly departing

The engine's functioning surprised me

The prisoner's being executed is unlikely

The war's having been declared is a fact.

The a-paraphrase, on the other hand, passes with flying colors:

I mentioned that he had suddenly departed

That the engine functioned surprised me

It is unlikely that the prisoner will be executed

It is a fact that the war has been declared.

Thus we cannot avoid the impression that there is a current change in the language towards substituting e nominals for d nominals in most contexts. The morphological gain is obvious. e's, being more noun-like, are more manageable as nominals; after all, the purpose of nominalization is to turn a sentence into a noun-phrase. And (e) does this more thoroughly than (d), which, really, is a case of arrested development. Yet the conceptual distinction represented by d versus e can be saved by virtue of (α): the a-form remains available either immediately, or as a paraphrase for e in d-containers. Thus we can formulate the following paraphrastic transformation:

$$(\beta) \quad Ct_d (e_i) \quad \Rightarrow \quad Ct_d (a_i)$$

where e_i and a_i are products of the same matrix.

Yet there are some cases in which the $Ct_d (e)$ form sounds inadequate. Consider:

? John's beautiful singing of the Marseillaise is unlikely. I think that the oddity of this sentence is due to the fact it is ambiguous with respect to (β). (β) can result in:

It is unlikely that John sang the Marseillaise beautifully

or in any of the following:

...that John can sing...
...that John would sing...
...that John will sing...

etc. e, as we know, loses tenses and modalities, d, on the other hand, at least saves *have* and *be able to*. Thus, either of

John's being able to sing the Marseillaise beautifully is unlikely

or

John's having sung the Marseillaise beautifully is unlikely

is preferable to *e*. *a*, of course, is the clearest of all. As far as I can see, there is only one kind of container in which certain d's cannot be substituted by a's or e's; e.g.:

He based his hopes upon John's having found the treasure
He did not reckon with her being able to get married so quickly.

Here a is unavailable (...P n container) and e would lose the tense or modality, rendering, thereby, the compound ambiguous.

Yet even here the *a*-form becomes available as soon as a noun like *fact* or *possibility* is added.

(β), of course, presupposes the notion of a *d*-container. Consequently, its full meaning will only unfold in the chapter that will classify containers.

IV. INCOMPLETE NOMINALS

1. The example we quoted above:

    He shocked us by telling a dirty joke

represents a generally productive pattern; the subject of a *d*-nominal can be dropped if it is identical with the subject of the container. Other examples:

    He based his hopes upon winning the race
    He escaped by disguising himself
    I recall having shaved myself
    I admit having seen her

etc. *Himself* and *myself* reflect the deleted subjects, which have to be the same as the subjects of the containers. Indeed,

    *I recall having shaved himself

is ungrammatical. Thus we have the schema,

$$N_i V... [N_i\text{'s } V_{ing} +] \rightarrow N_i \; V... [V_{ing} +]$$

This, however, remains an optional move and $N_i\text{'s}$ can be replaced without any structural change:

    He shocked us by his telling a dirty joke
    I recall my having seen her.

There are, on the other hand, nominalizing transformations that are based upon a noun-sharing between the container and the matrix in such a way that the missing occurrence cannot be replaced without structural change. I submit that this is the case in the following compounds:

    (1) I started writing letters

(2) I saw him die

(3) He wanted to go

(4) I ordered him to go.

The reflexive test, with -*self* works in every case:

I started shaving myself

I saw him kill himself

He wanted to save himself

I ordered him to shave himself

versus

*I started shaving himself

etc. Then it is clear that (1)-(4) fall into a consistent pattern: the subject of the matrix has to be identical with either the subject or the object of the container. Thus for (1) and (3) we get the elements

(5) N_i V $\bigcirc$; N_i V+

and for (2) and (4)

(6) N_i V $[N_j...]$; N_j V+

This last one is a real borderline case. N_j is in the accusative; thus we get the impression that it is the true object of N_i V. In that case, of course, N_i V would not be a container at all, and the result would be a relative-clause construction. But this is not the case. For, e.g.,

I saw him die

I ordered him to go

cannot be paraphrased by

I saw him who died

I ordered him who went

or something similar. If we want to paraphrase we have to resort to some kind of nominal, for instance

I saw his death

I ordered him that he should go.

It appears, then, that N_j in (6) is, as it were, only a half-object of $N_i V$, to be completed by a nominalization of the verb-phrase of the matrix: $V+$ or *to* $V+$.

The question still remains why the elements in (5) yield different structures in (1) and (3), and the elements in (6) yield different structures in (2) and (4). And, a connected question, is there any reason why (3) and (4) should be similar in having *to V+* rather than $V_{ing}+$ or $V+$ as in (1) and (2)? I offer the following hypothesis: while $V_{ing}+$ and $V+$ corresponds to the indicative in the matrix, *to V+* is the result of a subjunctive or subjunctive-equivalent in the matrix.[1] Thus I propose the following four nominalizing transformations to be discussed in the sequel:

(f) $N_i V_i \bigcirc; N_i V_j + \rightarrow N_i V_i [V_{j\ ing} +]$
(g) $N_i V_i [N_j...]; N_j V_j + \rightarrow (N_i V_i [N_j) V_j +]$
(h) $N_i V_i \bigcirc; N_i \text{ subj } (V_j) + \rightarrow N_i V_i [\text{to } V_j +]$
(i) $N_i V_i [N_j...]; N_j \text{ subj } (V_j) + \rightarrow (N_i V_i [N_j) \text{ to } V+]$

In (a)-(e) we could give the nominalizations without any specific container structures. Here the nominalizations operate only in connection with such structures. For this reason I call (f)-(i) incomplete nominalizations, and the nominals they produce (which appear in the brackets on the right hand side) incomplete nominals. To these I shall refer as *f, g*, etc.

2. The container class appropriate to (f) is a small one: *begin, start, keep, resume, continue, stop* and *finish*. The verb-phrase of the matrix retains its verb-like complements:

> I started singing the song
> He kept going
> She resumed sobbing fitfully.

In spite of this, *f* has nothing to do with *d*. N_i's cannot be inserted:

> *I started my singing the song
> *He kept his going.

Moreover, the paraphrase of *f* is not an *a* but an *e*:

> I started my singing of the song
> She resumed her fitful sobbing

and not

---

[1]   Instead of the straight subjunctive (*...that he go home*) the "subjunctive-equivalent", *should V +* (*...that he should go home*), is increasingly used. See E. Patridge, *The Concise Usage and Abusage* (New York, 1955), pp. 179ff.

*I started that I sing

etc. Hence we have, in most cases, the paraphrastic transformation

(γ) $f \Rightarrow e$

The only exception is *keep*:

*He kept his going.

But we can save this by inserting *up*:

He kept up his going.

Start, *keep*, and *stop*, but not the others, tolerate an alien subject in the nominals:

The police stopped the mob's rioting

The conductor started the singing of the choir

He kept the door open.

With some of these verbs, there is an inclination to use *to* $V+$ for $V_{ing}+$. E.g.:

I started to run

He began to drink.

These "backlash" forms are part of a fairly wide pattern of overlap between *to* $V+$ and $V_{ing} +$ to be discussed later.

3.   The result of (g) is a relatively rare but interesting form. Examples:

(7)   I heard him sing

(8)   I saw him cross the street

(9)   I felt the house tremble violently.

The container class is again a narrow one; it is confined to "perceptual" verbs like *see*, *hear*, *feel*, *watch*, and perhaps a few others. *g* has a passive form too, which is still less frequent:

(10) I saw him killed by the police

(11) I felt the line pulled.

Thus we have an offspring of (g):

(ga) $N_i V_i [N_j...]$; N_j is $V_{j \text{ en}} \rightarrow (N_i V_i [N_j]) V_{j \text{ en}}]$

Morphologically, a *g*-compound is similar to sentences like

(12) I let him pick flowers

(13) I made her cry.

The difference, however, can be seen as we realize that *g* easily goes into *e*, but a parallel move is impossible for (12)-(13). For (7)-(11) we get paraphrases:

> I heard his singing
> I saw his crossing of the street
> I felt the violent trembling of the house
> I saw his killing by the police
> I felt the pulling of the line.

For (12)-(13) we would get:

> *I let his picking of flowers
> *I made her crying.

The paraphrase just used is this:

> (δ) $g \Rightarrow e$

(δ) is useful for another purpose too. Take the sentences:

> (14) I saw him crossing the street
> (15) I saw him dying.

These are ambiguous sentences. One sense is the same as

> I saw him cross the street
> I saw him die.

Another sense can be paraphrased as follows:

> I saw him while (or when) he was crossing the street
> I saw him while (or when) he was dying.

This becomes clear as we select other host sentences:

> I spotted him crossing the street
> I found him dying.

Now these cannot go into *g*:

> *I spotted him cross the street
> *I found him die

nor into *e*:

> *I spotted his crossing of the street
> *I found his death.

But they have the paraphrase:

> I spotted him while he was crossing the street
> I found him when he was dying.

On the contrary

> I felt him trembling

has the *g*- and *e*- transforms:

I felt him tremble

I felt his trembling

but not the other kind:

? I felt him when he was trembling.

Then it is clear that $N_i\ V_i\ N_j\ V_{j\ ing} +$ is a variant of *g* if V_i is a *g*-container verb. If, however, V_i is not a *g*-container verb (like *spot, find*), then $N_i\ V_i\ N_j\ V_{j\ ing} +$ is a deletion result of a conjunction $N_i V N_j$ *while/when* N_j *be* $V_{ing} +$, and does not contain a nominal at all. (14)-(15) are ambiguous because the host, *I saw*, may or may not be a *g*-container; think of

I saw him die

versus

I saw him.

Semantic reasons may eliminate one branch of this ambiguity. Take:

I saw him dying, but I left before he died

cannot be paraphrased as

*I saw him die, but I left before he died.

The paraphrase will be

I saw him when he was dying but I left before he died.

Sentences like

He sent the ball flying

are clearly resolvable into a conjunction with a shared noun:

He sent the ball so that the ball is (or went) flying.

Here, too, *g* is impossible:

*He sent the ball fly

and so is (δ):

*He sent the flying of the ball.

4. As (f) is to (g), so is (h) to (i). While (h) is based on a noun-sharing between the subject of the container and the subject of the matrix, (i) is based upon a noun-sharing between the half-object of the container and the subject of the matrix. But *h* and *i* have *to V+* instead of $V_{ing} +$ or $V+$.

I suggested above that the use of *to V+* in the nominal corresponds to the presence of a subjunctive in the matrix. This is clear in *h*-compounds. The container class is made up of the verbs: *want, wish, like, prefer, decide, resolve, promise, remember, forget,* etc.; e.g.:

> I want to go home
> He likes to drive fast
> She decided to take the job
> He promised to pay on time
> She remembered to write to mother
> I forgot to shut the door.

Reflexives bring out the hidden subject:

> She promised to behave herself
> I forgot to shave myself.

Except for compounds with *want* and *like*, the *a*-transform is always possible:

> She decided that she should take the job
> He promised that he would pay on time
> I forgot that I should shut the door.

Here, as usual, we operate with subjunctive-equivalents. In some cases we may resort to the straight subjunctive. Take

> I wish to be in Paris
> He preferred to do the job.

The *a*-transforms are:

> I wish that I were in Paris
> He preferred that he do the job.

Even *want* and *like* permit somewhat clumsy *a*-transforms:

> ? I want (it) that I go home
> ? He likes (it) that he be respected.

This gives us the paraphrase:

> (ε) $h \Rightarrow a$ [subj (V)]

We must not forget that *remember* and *forget* are also *d*-containers. Compare:

> (16) I forgot shutting the door
> (17) I forgot to shut the door.

(16) results from deleting *my* from the *d*-nominal. By (α) it goes into

> I forgot that I (had) shut the door.

(17), on the other hand, has an *a*-transform according to (ε):

> I forgot that I should shut the door.

Accordingly, taking into consideration the semantics of *forget*, (16) implies that I did, while (17) implies that I did not shut the door. Unfortunately, due to the all pervading confusion of *to V+* and V_{ing} +, even (16) can be understood in the sense of (17). That the "backlash" operates here too, is obvious from the possibility of sentences like

> He likes driving a Cadillac
>
> I prefer doing the job myself

etc.

5. (i), as we said, is applicable in the case of a noun-sharing between the half-object of the container and the subject of the matrix. The relevant container-verbs are as follows: *ask, urge, order, advise, permit, compel, force, help*, etc. Some examples:

> I asked him to do the job
>
> I ordered him to arrest her
>
> He permitted me to go home

etc.

Except for *compel, force*, and *help*, the *i*'s are transformable into *a*'s:

> I asked (him) that he should do the job
>
> I ordered (him) that he should arrest her
>
> He permitted (me) that I go home.

As we see, the *a*-transform contains the subjunctive, or a subjunctive-equivalent. *Him* and *me* correspond to the half-objects we found in the *i*-form. The *a*-transforms are somewhat clumsy. Still clumsier are some *d*-forms, yet they occur:

> I advised his accepting the job
>
> He permitted my going home

etc. The tendency that generated (β) operates here too. *e*-forms can supplant *d*-forms.

I advised his acceptance of the job

I ordered her arrest.

Some of these offbeat forms lack the immediacy characteristic of *i*. Compare:

(18) The judge ordered the sheriff to arrest her

(19) The judge ordered the sheriff that he should arrest her

(20) The judge ordered that the sheriff should arrest her

(21) The judge ordered her arrest by the sheriff.

Now suppose that the judge ordered the district attorney to ask the sheriff to arrest her. In this case (20)-(21) will be true, but not (18)-(19). So while (19) is a paraphrase of (18), (20)-(21) are not. For this reason I prefer to think that most *i*-containers double as *d*-containers (with the usual *e*-forms and *a*-paraphrases).

Some containers of the *h*-group also tolerate half-objects and then, to some extent, imitate the *i*-constructions; e.g.:

(22) I wanted him to be here

(23) I preferred him to do the job

etc. This possibility is restricted to *want, wish, prefer* and perhaps *like*. Even for these verbs, however, the *i*-construction lacks some of the potentialities it normally has. While, for example,

I ordered him to go

undergoes the passive:

He has been ordered by me to go

(22) and (23) hardly tolerate the move:

*He has been wanted by me to be here

? He has been preferred by me to do the job.

Again, genuine *i*-containers can be reflexive:

I permitted myself to take liberties

He forced himself to eat fish.

h-containers cannot:

(24) I wanted myself to be here

(25) I preferred myself to do the job.

It will be objected that (24) and (25) pass. True, but then *myself* is emphatic subject and not object. This appears as we consider the transform of (24)

I wanted to be here myself
versus, e.g.,

*I permitted to take liberties myself.

I conclude, then, that *h*-container verbs naturally assume the identity of two subjects and the insertion of a foreign subject, even when possible, remains indigestible transformationally.

6.   In the compounds resulting from (f)-(i) the nominal appeared as the object (or "second-half-object") of the container. And the noun-sharing between the matrix and the container involved the subject or the half-object of the container. It would seem to be obvious that other types of containers, like ○ *is A*, for instance, cannot participate in nominalizations based on noun-sharing between the matrix and the container, which, as we saw, usually produce *to V+* or V_{ing} + nominals. Yet there is a quite important nominalization achieving exactly this result. What happens is that the ○ *is A* (or ○ *is N*) container obtains a genuine noun connected by the prepositions *for* or *of*; e.g. (using *it*-extractions freely):

It is impossible for him to solve the problem

To be a chairman is a burden for him

It was stupid of him to take that job.

For reasons of transformational behavior I divide the transformations producing these compounds as follows:

(j) N_i V+; ○ is A (or N) for N_i → [to V+] is A (or N) for N_i

(k) N_i V+; ○ is A of N_i → [to V+] is A of N_i

The adjective-class corresponding to (j) comprises *easy, difficult, possible*, and *impossible, necessary, superfluous*, etc. The class of container-nouns is not easy to define; it will contain *task, duty, burden, work*, and so forth, more often than not with appropriate adjectives; e.g.:

To build a battleship is a difficult task for any shipyard.

To study mathematics is a burden for him.

For N_i can be dropped if the context makes N_i redundant; e.g.:

He found the razor and then it was easy to shave himself
I learned the language and then it was possible to understand the text.
In want of such context, *for somebody*, or *for anybody*, should
be replaced:

It is impossible to learn Chinese in two months
It is difficult to please everybody.

j-adjectives permit the following transformation:

(26) to VN_j is A → N_j is A to V—

e.g.:

To please him is easy → He is easy to please
To solve this problem is impossible → This problem is impossible to solve.

In this latter case *impossible* can be shifted into prenominal
position in two steps:

This problem is an impossible problem to solve → This is
an impossible problem to solve

Thus, we circumvent the impossibility of inserting an adjective
into a definite noun-phrase (see Chapter I).

(26) indicates that a *j*-container adjective can be ascribed to
the object of the matrix directly. This is the point at which *k*-
container adjectives part company. For these can be ascribed
directly not to the object but to the subject of the container. Take
the transformations:

To take that job was stupid of him → He was stupid to take
that job
It was not nice of him to offend the lady → He was not nice
to offend the lady

i.e.:

(27) to V+ is A of N_i → N_i is A to V+

The class of *k*-adjectives is easy to collect: *clever, stupid, nice,
kind, good, awful*, etc.

k-compounds are transformable into *a*-compound with more or
less success:

It is stupid of him that he should take that job
It is nice of him that he should visit her mother.

And so are some *j*-compounds:

>It is possible for him that he join the class
>
>It is unnecessary for you that you should apologize.

Mark the subjunctive in all these forms. Some other *j*-compounds, notably the ones with *easy* and *difficult*, refuse the *a*-paraphrase;

>*It is easy for him that he should learn Chinese
>
>*It is difficult for me that I run a mile in four minutes.

These adjectives, however, take the *e*-form easily:

>The learning of that language was easy for him
>
>Life in China is difficult.

The simple V_{ing} + backlash, on the other hand, works throughout:

>Joining the class is possible for him
>
>Solving the problem was easy for me
>
>Helping the poor is a duty
>
>Walking is hardly necessary these days
>
>Taking that job was stupid of him

etc.

7. The uncertainty between *to* $V+$ and V_{ing} + corresponds, I think, to the uncertainty affecting the use of the subjunctive in general. Indeed, it can be shown that we accept *to* $V+$ instead of V_{ing} + more readily if the container does not clearly require the indicative in the matrix, and we accept V_{ing} + instead of *to* $V+$ more readily if the container does not clearly indicate the subjunctive in the matrix.

Consider *f*-compounds. It is primarily with *begin* and *start* that *to* $V+$ tends to supersede $V_{ing}+$; e.g.:

>(28) He started to say something
>
>(29) He began to hesitate

are at least as good as

>He started saying something
>
>He began hesitating.

The fact that (28) and (29) do not entail the indicative of the matrix can be shown by the failure of the *e*-paraphrase:

     *He started the saying of something

     ? He began his hesitation.

Now contrast this with *resume*:

     ?He resumed to dig the hole

is hardly acceptable for

     He resumed digging the hole.

But here the *e*-form is all right:

     He resumed the digging of the hole.

Intuitively, we feel that while one can start to say something without actually saying something, one cannot resume digging without actually digging. This difference is, admittedly, vague. But so is the degree of permissibility of *to V+* for $V_{ing}+$.

g-compounds are generally free from the uncertainty; the "perceptual" quality of the containers requires an indicative matrix and permit a clear *e*-paraphrase. Thus

     *I saw him to cross the street

     *I felt him to shake

do not pass.

As to *h*-verbs, it is *like* that caters to the $V_{ing}+$:

     I like travelling

     He likes driving a Cadillac.

This, again, is due to the simple semantical fact that while one can want, decide, resolve, promise to do something without actually doing it, one can hardly be said to like doing something without actually doing it. Thus *like* implies the indicative and permits the $V_{ing}+$ form. The others resist with more or less force:

     *I wanted going home

     ?I decided driving a Cadillac

     ?He promised paying $5

Among the *i*-verbs, it is *help* that admits $V_{ing}+$ without oddity:

     I helped him building the house

     He helped me escaping.

The others much less:

     *I asked him going with me

     *I ordered him going home.

Accordingly, it is *help*, above the rest, that most likely implies actual performance. Incidentally, *help* exhibits a curious "hang-over" of g:

I helped him build a house

I helped him escape.

j- and k-adjectives (and nouns) are quite open to both forms, since they generally leave the question of actual performance open. Yet even here, for instance,

To free the slaves would have been impossible

sounds better than

Freeing the slaves would have been impossible.

On the other hand,

Freeing the slaves was easy

is as good as

To free the slaves was easy.

Finally, the confusion of $V_{ing}+$ and $to\ V+$ can affect complete nominals as well. We recall that some a-containers fail as d-containers:

I know that he is here

I believe that God exists

do not go into

*I know his being here

*I believe God's existence.

The situation, of course, can be remedied by inserting *of* or *in*. The point, however, is that we can supplement the missing d by a pseudo-i with a somewhat questionable result:

?I know him to be here

?I believe God to exist.

Containers that are suited to d, like *mention*, *deny*, etc., do not accept this:

*I denied him to be here

*He mentioned me to come.

Here there is no need for a substitute; d is available:

I denied his being here

He mentioned my coming.

The same confusion can affect a-d container adjectives like *unlikely* and produce results like:

?It is unlikely for him to arrive

?He is unlikely to arrive before noon.

8. *h* and *i* have negative counterparts as it appears from the following examples:

(30) I refrained from hurting the man

(31) He abstained from eating meat

(32) I restrained him from acting foolishly

(33) He prevented me from going home.

Intuition tells us that, in spite of the $V_{ing}+$, (30)-(31) are more akin to the products of (h) than of (f), and that (32)-(33) are more similar to the products of (i) than of (g). After all, (30)-(33) do not imply performance; on the contrary. Hence the matrix is not likely to have an indicative form. Yet it is not easy to show this transformationally. We have to resort to substandard forms and analogies to do so. Compare:

I forbade him to go out

I prohibited him from going out.

Now there are substandard forms crossing the line:

?I forbade him from going out

?I prohibited him to go out.

And they both can be forced into the *a*-mold with a subjunctive:

?I forbade it that he should go out

?I prohibited it that he should go out.

Hence I conclude that *from* $V_{ing}+$ is in general a counterpart of *to* $V+$. Looking at it this way we get:

(h_a) $N_i\ V_i\ \bigcirc$; N_i subj $(V_j)+\ \rightarrow\ N_i\ V_i$ [from $V_{j\ ing}\ +$]

(i_a) $N_i\ V_i\ [N_j...]$; N_j subj $(V_j)+\ \rightarrow\ (N_i\ V_i\ [N_j)$ from $V_{j\ ing}\ +$]

Then *refrain* and *abstain* will be h_a-containers, and *restrain, prevent, prohibit,* etc., will be i_a-containers.

An interesting comparison: the completion of *NVN to...* or *NVN from...* may require a simple noun or a $V+$ resp. $V_{ing}+$. Take

(34) I introduce you to...

(35) I drive you from...

(36) I told you to...

(37) I prevent you from....

John and *the house* can complete (34) and (35), *go away* and *going away* can complete (36) and (37), and not the other way around. *Introduce* and *drive* are not containers, but *tell* and *prevent* are.

9. (c), as we recall, nominalized a sentence by substituting *wh...* for one of its elements. If, in addition, the container shares a noun with the subject of the matrix, a *to V—* version becomes possible, provided, once more, that the matrix is in the subjunctive rather than in the indicative; e.g.:

He knows what to eat

Whom to elect is the problem (for us)

I asked him what to eat

I told him what to eat

What to do is not easy (for us) to tell.[2]

The relevant paraphrases show the noun-sharing and the subjunctive in the matrix:

He knows what he should eat

I wonder how I should solve the problem

Whom we should elect is the problem (for us)

etc. The indicative would not do:

He knows what he eats

etc. Thus, in general,

$$(c_a) \quad Ct(N_i) \text{ [wh... } N_i \text{ subj (V...)]} \rightarrow Ct(N_i) \text{ [wh... to V...]}$$

The fascinating contrast,

(38) I asked him what to eat

(39) I told him what to eat

requires closer analysis. The obvious paraphrase of (38) is

I asked him what *I* should eat

[2] As the perceptive reader will realize, this example is the result of two nominalizations, (j) and (c), and the application of (c_a).

but that of (39) is

    I told him what *he* should eat.

Why is this so? I think that the answer depends on two differences between *ask* and *tell*. In the first place *tell*, but not *ask*, requires the half-object before the nominal:

    I ask what I should eat

    *I tell what I should eat.

This point is connected with another one. *Ask* is a question-container, *tell* is not:

    I ask: what should I eat?

    *I tell (you): what should I eat?

Now most of the *i*-containers are like *tell* in these respect (*order, force, compel, permit*, etc.). Thus *tell* at once gravitates toward the *i*-mold: (39) is resolved into

    I told him to eat N

with the paraphrase

    I told him that he should eat N.

Ask, on the other hand, tends toward the question-form: so (38) is interpreted as

    I asked (him): should I eat N_1 or N_2 or... etc.

Consequently *what* after *tell* replaces a specific N, but after *ask* it replaces an alternation of N's. This is a general difference between *i*-containers and "question" -containers.

    I ordered him what to eat

can be completed by adding *namely meat;*

    I wonder what to eat

cannot be thus completed. An alternation is required: *meat or something else.* Indeed, even *ask* tends to be an *i*-container if the noun is specific:

    I asked him what to eat, namely meat

should be paraphrased as

    I asked him what *he* should eat, namely meat.

If an alternation is added, the picture changes:

    I asked him what to eat; meat or something else

must be interpreted as

    I asked him what I should eat: meat or something else.

Tell admits specification:

I told him what to eat, namely meat

but rejects the alternation:

*I told him what to eat; meat or something else.

To conclude: *what* after *ask* replaces an alternation of nouns which precludes the interpretation of *ask* as an *i*-container. Since, moreover, the connection of *ask* to the subject (*I* in (38)) is stronger than the connection to the object (*him* in (38)), which can be deleted, *I* wins out in the reconstructed matrix. *Tell*, on the other hand, at once decides in favor of *i* and, thus, for *he* in the matrix of (39).

As *c* has a *to V+* version in c_a, so *b* has a *to V+* version according to

(b$_a$) $Ct(N_i)$ [whether N_i subj $(V+)$] $\rightarrow$ $Ct(N_i)$ [whether to $V+$].

Examples:

I wonder whether to go (or not)

I advised him whether to go (or not)

Whether to go or not is the problem (for us).

Whether may be omitted in this latter case.

To go or not is the problem

To be or not to be, that is the question.

V. CONTAINERS

1. On the basis of the previous discussion, the notion of a container should be fairly clear and, in particular with respect to incomplete nominals, some distinct container classes have already emerged. Yet it is desirable that we should collect the pieces and present a systematic account. This is especially necessary in connection with d- and e-nominals, since their transformational behavior is a function of the container contexts.

I shall classify containers according to two principles: structure, and co-occurrence restriction, with respect to the nominals they are able to receive. And I introduce the following terminology: the containers will be divided into "types" according to the diversity of structure, and into "classes" according to the variety of co-occurrence restriction. The result, of course, will be a cross-classification, since, as we saw in many examples, a container type may occur in many classes, and a class may extend to many types.

The container types resemble the most common forms of elementary sentence. If we represent the noun-gap as "$\bigcirc$", we get

$$Ct^{V-} \quad : \quad NV \bigcirc$$
$$Ct^{V+} \quad : \quad \bigcirc V+$$
$$Ct^{A} \quad : \quad \bigcirc \text{ is A}$$
$$Ct^{N} \quad : \quad \bigcirc \text{ is N}$$
$$Ct^{P} \quad : \quad ...P \bigcirc$$

Now each of these types can take nominals of various classes. These latter I indicate by appropriate suffixes; e.g.:

Ct_a^{V-} : I think [that she arrived]

Ct_{ad}^{V-} : I mentioned $\begin{cases}\text{[that she arrived]}\\\text{[her arrival]}\end{cases}$

Ct_{adh}^{V-} : I forgot $\begin{cases}\text{[that she arrived]}\\\text{[her arrival]}\\\text{[to visit her]}\end{cases}$

Ct_i^{V-} : I ordered [him to go]

Ct_{ha}^{V-} : He abstained [from voting]

Ct_e^{V-} : He watched [the execution]

Ct_{ad}^{V+} : $\begin{cases}\text{[That she arrived]}\\\text{[Her arrival]}\end{cases}$ surprised me

Ct_e^{V+} : [The fight] lasted for an hour

Ct_{ad}^{A} : $\begin{cases}\text{[Her death]}\\\text{[That she died]}\end{cases}$ is unlikely

Ct_e^{A} : [The erosion of the hill] was gradual

Ct_j^{A} : [To win the race] was easy for him

Ct_{adj}^{A} : $\begin{cases}\text{[That he won the race]}\\\text{[His winning the race]}\\\text{(For him) [to win the race]}\end{cases}$ is impossible

Ct_{ad}^{N} : $\begin{cases}\text{[That he died]}\\\text{[His death]}\end{cases}$ is a fact

Ct_e^{N} : [The erosion] was a slow process

Ct_j^{N} : [To help the poor] is a duty

Ct_d^{P} : I counted upon [his winning the race]

Ct_e^{P} : I talked about [the performance]

etc. With respect to *h-i*-containers, I shall not add other suffixes (like *a* or *d*), if the matrix must contain the subjunctive, e.g., *resolve* will be a Ct_h^{V-} only, in spite of the possibility of

He resolved that he should help her

because indicative matrices fail:

*He resolved that he helped her.

Forget, on the other hand, will be a Ct_{adh}^{V-} because it tolerates indicative matrixes, as in

He forgot that she has arrived

He forgot her arrival.

In these last lines I took the liberty of referring to individual
verbs (like *resolve* or *forget*) as containers, which is at variance
with our previous practice of calling containers only sentence-
roots with a noun-gap. It is obvious, however, that the V is the
crucial feature of a Ct^{V+} or Ct^{V-}, the A is the decisive feature
of a Ct^A, the N of a Ct^N. The remaining elements are immaterial
for our purposes. Thus, for instance, the Ct_{ad}^{V+}, ○ *surprise...N...*
has all the varieties of

    ○ surprised me
    ○ will surprise you greatly
    ○ surprises naive folks

etc. But our concern will be restricted to the kind of nominal the
verb takes in all such occurrences. And with respect to this task
the variations just mentioned are irrelevant. Not even the semantically interesting fact that the object of *surprise* must be a "human"
(or at least "animal") noun-phrase is within the scope of our in-
quiry.

2.   It cannot be the purpose of the present study to give a complete or nearly complete list of all containers. What I shall do
is to select paradigm-groups that are representative of the rest and
explain the principles of selection, so that the completion of the
task may become possible within the framework of setting up a
structural and transformational dictionary of the language.

In this sense, I shall start presently, *in medias res*, by collecting
the paradigm group for the classes Ct_a and Ct_d. (α), in Chapter
III, is enough to show the affinity and the considerable overlap
between these two classes. Indeed, while Ct_{ad}'s abound there are
only few exclusive Ct_a's, and exclusive Ct_d's are restricted to the
type Ct^P.

For the wide variety of Ct_{ad}'s the following sample, collected
according to container-types, will be sufficient.

    Ct_{ad}^{V+} : *surprise, astonish, shock, imply, entail, indicate;*
    Ct_{ad}^{V-} : *mention, deny, admit, recall, remember, forget,*
           expect, anticipate;

Ct_{ad}^{A} : *likely, probable, possible, certain* and opposites;
Ct_{ad}^{N} : *fact, result, reason, cause, axiom, idea.*

I add the exclusively Ct_a's:

Ct_a^{V-} : *think, believe, know, hope;*
Ct_a^{A} : *true, false;*
Ct_a^{N} : *statement, proposition.*

Ct_d^{P}'s, as we remember, defy (α), so they cannot be Ct_a's.

The collection of Ct_{ad}'s is a relatively easy task. All we have to do is to form a battery consisting of *a*, and several versions of the *d*-form exhibiting verb-like complements, and test the container in question against it. To exclude semantic incompatibilities, we might have to use batteries derived from various matrices. One battery, for instance, may be the following:

that he sang the Marseillaise
his having sung the Marseillaise
his not having sung the Marseillaise
his being able to sing the Marseillaise
his singing the Marseillaise aloud.

The fact that nearly all Ct_{ad}'s can receive nominals that are morphologically *e*'s, like

his singing of the Marseillaise
the beautiful singing

etc., should not disturb us, nor should it prompt us to add the suffix *e*. We shall regard as genuine *e*-containers only those that cannot receive *d*-forms, and, in particular, that refuse (β). Thus, for instance, in spite of the fact that *surprise* takes an *e*, as in

His sudden death surprised us

surprise is not a Ct_e because it lets in things like

That he died surprised us
His having died surprised us
His not having died surprised us

and so forth. A real Ct_e, like *occur*, is restricted to the *e*-form:

His sudden death occurred at noon

and refuses the *a*- and *d*-forms:

*That he died suddenly occurred at noon
*His having died occurred at noon
*His not having died occurred at noon

and the like. I repeat: while Ct_{ed} are "loose" containers, Ct_e's are "tight" ones. The former permit morphological e's, but then these are paraphraseable into a. The latter do not receive a's or d's at all.

An indirect proof of the homogeneity of the Ct_{ad}-class can be gathered by reflecting upon their mutual compatibility. Facts, results, reasons, etc., can be mentioned, admitted or denied, they can surprise, shock or astonish us, they can imply or indicate other things, and, finally, they can be described as likely, probable or possible. True, there are some semantic incompatibilities (like *false fact*), but the "family", by and large, hangs together. And, as we shall see, Ct_e's form another, quite distinct, family.

The nominal compounds generated from Ct_{ad}'s undergo the usual transformations, like the passive, as in

Her arrival is expected by the crowd
She has been shocked by their shouting

etc. Ct_a^{V-} compounds refuse the passive, due to the impossibility of Ct_a^P :

*I was surprised by that she came.

The d-form has to jump into the breach:

I was surprised by her coming.

Questions and *wh*-pronominalizations go smoothly:

What do you expect? That she'll come.

Her arrival, which was unexpected, shocked the crowd

and so forth. There are some special transformations in addition. Ct_a^A - and Ct_a^N - compounds permit the *it*-extraction:

(1) a is A $\rightarrow$ it is A a
(2) a is N $\rightarrow$ it is N a

e.g.:

It is unlikely that she came
It is possible that it'll rain

It is a fact that she arrived

It is the result of long planning that he won the election

It is his idea that the Chinese are behind the revolt

It is an axiom that all men are equal.

Cause is somewhat reluctant, yet can be made to conform:

It was the cause and not the result of the depression that public confidence in the economy declined.

Fact, *axiom* and *idea* permit the following:

(3) d is N → the N of d

e.g.:

the fact of his arrival

the axiom of the identity of indiscernibles.

Result, *reason*, *cause* do not follow (3) for an obvious reason. *Of*, explicitly or implicitly, must follow them anyway as part of a genitive structure. Results, etc., are results of something else, unlike facts, etc. What is interesting for us is the fact that this "something else", too, has to be given in terms of a nominal. Ordinary nouns will not do:

*The depression was the result of Hoover

?Hoover was the cause of the depression, etc.

Thus we arrive at the notion of a double-container. *Result*, for instance, stands between two a's or d's. Examples like

His not seeing the red light was the result of having drunk five Martinis

show this beyond doubt. We realize that certain verbs are also double containers. *Cause* for instance:

His not seeing the red light caused the crash.

In this case, I think, the first nominal has to be an a or d, the second an e; facts, for one thing, can cause things, but cannot be caused:

The fact that he did not see the red light caused the crash

?His not seeing the red light caused the fact that he rammed the truck.

Finally Ct_{ad}^N's (and Ct_e^N's) can be simply apposited to a's; e.g.:

the fact that he came

the idea that she might win

his statement that the president is incapable.

Thus we have:

(4) a is N → the N a.

3. The collection of Ct_e's will proceed along the lines mentioned in connection with Ct_{ad}'s. Here the battery of compatible forms is a simple one: various e's exhibiting noun-like complements; e.g.:

his singing of the Marseillaise

his beautiful singing

the singing.

Then, from among the containers that fit these forms, we weed out the ones that can take the a- and d-forms as well. The residue will be the class of Ct_e's.

For a paradigm e-group I suggest the following:

Ct_e^{V+} : *occur, takes place, takes (up)(time),*
start, being, last, end, procede, follow;

Ct_e^{V-} : *see, hear, feel, watch, observe,*
follow, notice, imitate;

Ct_e^A : *slow, fast, sudden, gradual, long, short*;

Ct_e^N : *process, event.*

Here, again, the indirect proof works within semantic limits. For it is processes and events (and not facts, results and the like) that can occur, take place, begin and end; they (and not facts or ideas) can be seen, heard, watched, followed and observed; and they (and not facts, etc.) are slow, fast, sudden or gradual.

It will be objected that, say, *see* or *observe* may take a's or d's as well (and, accordingly, one can see or observe facts or results). True, but this merely shows that these words are ambiguous. A little semantic exercise makes this clear.

Compare:

(5) He saw that the president must have arrived

(6) He saw the arrival of the president.

He saw in (6) but not in (5) may take adverbial phrases like *through the window in spite of the mist*. Again, *saw* in (5) may be paraphrased by *realized*, and *saw* in (6) by *watched*, but not the other way around. For these and similar reasons we know that *he saw* in (6) is an *e*-container, so that it is not subject to (β);

He saw that the president has arrived

is not a paraphrase of (6).

$Ct_e^{N'}$'s permit a transformation similar to (3):

(7) *e* is N → the N of *e*

Some products of (7):

the event of Caesar's assasination
the process of the erosion of the rock.

4. Almost all Ct_{ad}'s can take *c*'s. A few illustrations:

How he won the race indicated his thorough training
What I saw surprised me
I forgot what he gave me
What he saw was uncertain
What he ate was the reason for his upset stomach.

In many cases, however, the results are more or less odd:

Who sat on the throne surprised me
He mentioned who killed the grocer

or hardly acceptable:

?How he entered the house is a fact
?Whom he found there was improbable
?Who was the president was the cause of the revolt.

I suppose that the oddity of these and other similar sentences springs from a tendency to confuse *c* with the relative clause. Since the latter construction is far more common than the former, the listener is inclined to interpret *c* as if it were a relative clause. This move, of course, renders many of these sentences senseless. Only few informants see the difference, for instance, between

He who sat on the throne surprised me
Who sat on the throne surprised me.

At any rate, exclusive Ct_a's refuse *c*'s except *know*:

I know what he found

but

> *I think what he found
> *What he found is true.

Ct_d^P's admit c's as in

> He talked about how he did it.

Through this possibility some exclusive Ct_a's can be saved for c's, e.g.:

> I think of what I lost
> the statement of what I lost.

b's are more selective. As a sample of these "problematic" containers, I suggest the following:

> Ct_b^{V+} : *puzzle* (*worry, disturb*);
> Ct_b^{V-} : *ask* (*somebody*), *wonder, doubt*;
> Ct_b^{A} : *certain, uncertain*;
> Ct_b^{N} : *question, problem*.

All Ct_b's are also Ct_c's. Some of them, however, refuse a's; e.g.:

> *I wonder that he came
> *That he came is the question.

As to $Ct_f - Ct_j$, the discussion in the previous chapter will be sufficient.

5. The class of nouns, verbs and adjectives that are essentially containers is fairly well separated from the rest. True, there are some genuinely ambivalent words, which can function equally as containers and non-containers. We have encountered *see*, which is a Ct_{ad}^{V-}, yet, at the same time, it may take ordinary nouns as in

> I see the house

Similarly, *know*:

> I know the president.

Such ambivalence is not restricted to Ct^{V-}'s. Fights can be long but so can houses, albeit the first in time, the second in space.

In spite of a few such exceptions, however, the realm of containers remains well-defined. In order to appreciate this better, I add a few words about what I shall call crypto-nominals and suppressed nominals.

There is a group of nouns that do not have the morphological features of a nominal, yet they occur, more or less exclusively, in containers. *Wind, fire, tornado, noise, fair, supper, Mass, accident, war*, etc., are at home, quite consistently, in Ct_e's:

> The sudden wind started at noon
> I watched the accident which occurred in front of my house
> I heard the noise of the machine
> The tornado caused the fire
> The fair lasted for two weeks
> He followed the Mass on TV
> The war began immediately

etc. Intuition confirms this: we regard the referents of these nouns as events or processes rather than physical objects.

Finally, in many cases the verbal part of the nominal may be omitted. I claim that this is so in the following examples (container-element italicized):

> Flies are *impossible* in this climate
> The abominable snowman is a *fact*
> Hitler had a hypnotic *effect* on his audience
> Petroleum is the *result* of organic decomposition
> I *watched* the train
> I *heard* the plane
> I *felt* his heart
> John is *impossible*
> Mary *shocked* me

and so forth. In every one of these cases one can predict the existence of a sentence completing the nominal:

> [The existence of] flies is *impossible* in this climate
> [The existence of] the abominable snowman is a *fact*
> Hitler ['s speeches] had a hypnotic *effect* on his audience
> [The origin of] petroleum is the *result* of organic decomposition
> I *watched* the train [go by]
> I *heard* [the noise of] the plane
> I *felt* [the beating of] his heart
> John is *impossible* [to live with]
> Mary *shocked* me [by what she did].

Moreover, these sentences will be recognized by native speakers as paraphrases or true interpretations of the original ones. If, on the other hand, we exchange the container element for a non-container one, the sentences cannot be completed in the same manner. Take, for instance,

(8) [The ... of] the abominable snowman is an *animal*

(9) Hitler ['s ...] had a brown *coat*

(10) I *pushed* the train [...]

(11) John is *tall* [...]

(12) Mary *kissed* me [...].

The gaps in (8) and (9) require genuine nouns; *ancestor*, for instance, can complete (8), and *servant* fits into (9). But no nominal will do. (10) and (12) can acquire adverbial phrases, while (11) hardly anything. Nominals would be out of place again. The case of *watch* is instructive. This verb can take practically any noun for object. Yet, I think, it remains a container-verb (Ct_e^{V-}). For, although one can watch "immobile" objects like rocks or chairs, in saying things like

I watched the rock for half an hour

the speaker indicates that he expected something to happen there. No such implication is carried by

I sat on the rock for half an hour.

PART TWO

ADJECTIVES

VI. CLASSIFICATION OF ADJECTIVES

1. The most characteristic position in which adjectives occur is the prenominal one, i.e, between the article (or equivalent) and the noun, e.g.:

the *red* balloon

an *old* man

these *beautiful little* flowers

her *woolen* dress.

Since in such phrases A is an adjunct of N, the question arises concerning the transformational origin of the compound. An obvious solution would be to regard AN as a nominalization of the sentence N *is* A. It is clear, however, that AN cannot be a proper nominalization. In the first place, as a little reflection will show, the co-occurrence restrictions affecting the AN are almost the same as those affecting the N alone. If, for instance, N is an original noun and not a proper nominal, then neither N alone, nor AN will fit into containers. If, on the other hand, N is a nominal, then AN too will fit into the kind of container suitable for N. This is by no means the case with respect to a proper nominalization of the N *is* A matrix. As we know, there are two nominal products of this matrix, N's *being* A and *the A-ness of* N. These, of course, will fit into Ct_d's and Ct_e's respectively, which remain closed to the AN-compound. Using an illustration, while we can touch, pluck, tear apart roses and red roses, we cannot do these things to the redness of roses. On the contrary, while the redness of a rose can be caused by some chemical, roses or red roses are not caused by anything.

Another possibility of immediate derivation arises from the consideration of relative clauses: *AN* may come from *N wh...* *is A*. This possibility leads to a further question: is it the appositive or the restrictive clause that is the general source of *AN*-phrases? I am going to show that in an overwhelming majority of cases the restrictive clause is the immediate source.

I shall give three arguments. The first argument demonstrates that *AN* is equivalent to the restrictive *N that is A* in achieving identification. Consider the sequence:

(1) I see three roses. The red one is lovely.

and then compare:

(2) I see three roses. The one that is red is lovely.

(3) ?[I see three roses. The one, which is red, is lovely.]

Clearly, (2) is a paraphrase of (1). (3) becomes deviant, because the identification suggested by *the* is lacking. The *AN*, in (1), however, bears out *the* as much as the restrictive *N that is A* in (2).

The second argument is based upon the impossibility of adding a restrictive clause to an already definite noun-phrase.[1] Take the sequence:

?[I see a man. The tall man wears a hat.]

This sequence shows the same lack of continuity as the following:

?[I see a man. The man that is tall wears a hat.]

Using the appositive clause the discontinuity is overcome:

I see a man. The man, who is tall, wears a hat.

The same reason accounts for the otherwise baffling fact that proper names and personal pronouns usually do not take prenominal adjectives: *blond Joseph*, *tall Mary*, *fat you*, etc. This is clearly not due to co-occurrencerestrictions:

Joseph is blond

Mary is tall

You are fat

are correct. If an adjective still occurs in front of a proper name, then it should be interpreted either as selecting one among many possible referents, or an aspect of the same individual. But, as

---

[1] See Part One, I, 2.

we recall, the same possibilities are available to the restrictive clause even accompanied by *the*. Indeed,

    I met the tall Mary

is paraphraseable by

    I met the Mary that is tall

and, thus, clearly indicates a selection among many Mary's. Sentences like

    I prefer the late Rembrandt

may require a more complex, but fairly obvious resolution, once more along the lines of restrictive clauses.

The third argument draws a parallel between non-identifying restrictive clauses and AN-phrases. Compare:

    (4) Poisonous snakes are dangerous

    (5) Poisonous vipers are dangerous.

(5), unlike (4), sounds redundant for semantic reasons. The same redundancy echoes from

    (6) Vipers that are poisonous are dangerous.

The appositive construction in

    (7) Vipers, which are poisonous, are dangerous

avoids the redundancy. So (6), and not (7), is equivalent to (5).

For these reasons I conclude that in a great number of cases AN is nothing but a product of the restrictive N *wh... is A:*

    (A') AN ← N wh... is A

Yet there are many AN's for which the appositive clause appears to be the source. This is certainly true in case of "Homeric" epithets like *swift Achilles, blonde Here, long-haired Achaeans*, etc. More contemporary examples·

    And there goes *poor Joe*

    He is just an *arrogant German*

    Kill that *dirty rat!*

    A *poisonous viper* was hidden in the basket

and so forth. As we multiply the examples we get the impression that this device is restricted to poetic, rhetorical or at least emphatic use of language. Consequently, the existence of such liberty should not move us to reconsider (A') which is founded on much deeper and quite general arguments.

Examples, on the other hand, like
>(8) utter fool
>(9) nuclear scientist
>(10) beautiful dancer

and so on, represent a much more serious challenge. It is obvious that (8) and (9) cannot come from
>*fool who is utter
>?scientist who is nuclear

and that there is a sense of (10) that does not correspond to
>dancer who is beautiful.

Thus, I submit that (A') should be generalized as follows:
>(A) AN ← N wh... ...A...

leaving the structure of the restrictive clause open. As we shall see, this structure depends upon the particular A, which fact will afford us a classification of adjectives with further implications for their transformational behavior.

2.　Returning to the example mentioned above,
>beautiful dancer

it is quite clear that the phrase is ambiguous. One sense is exhibited by a straight application of (A'):
>beautiful dancer – dancer who is beautiful.

The other sense, however, can be made explicit by the following derivation:
>beautiful dancer – dancer who dances beautifully.

Both paths of derivation are obviously productive. Phrases like *red balloon, running water, broken pot, sad face,* and so forth, require the former path, while others like *fast runner, slow speaker, good dancer,* and so on, follow the second. Thus we get the transformations:
>(I) AN – N wh... is A

which marks the first way, and
>(III') $AN_V - N_V$ wh... VD_A[2]

which gives the second.

---

[2]　N_V here denotes the "agent"-nominal formed from V (usually by means of the suffix *-er*) and D_A the adverb formed from A (usually by means of the suffix *-ly*). The reason for the numbering, (III'), will appear later.

The interesting feature of (III') is the fact that the adjective is not ascribed to the subject absolutely, but only with respect to a verb which is morphologically recoverable from a noun ascribed to the same subject. If I say

She is a beautiful dancer

in the sense of (III'), I do not imply

She is beautiful.

If, on the other hand, I say the same sentence in the sense of (I), I do imply

She is beautiful.

For the same reasons a slow speaker may be a fast runner and good dancer a bad chess-player, and so on. A red apple, however, cannot be a green fruit or a blue object.

Beautiful, as we saw, fits into both (I) and (III'). Such ambivalence is not displayed by many adjectives. *Red* is confined to (I), and *fast* to (III'). The former is obvious as soon as we realize that *red* has no adverbial derivative, the second is clear due to the fact that a fast dancer can be a slow speaker. These points lead us to an interesting experiment. Take the sentences:

    (11)   She is a blonde and beautiful dancer

    (12)   She is a slow and beautiful dancer

    (13) *She is a blonde and slow dancer.

To our surprise *beautiful* ceases to be ambiguous in (11) and (12), while (13) becomes deviant. The reason is as follows: *blonde* is confined to (I), so the force of conjunction with *beautiful* interprets the latter as a member of (I) too; *slow* is restricted to (III'), so by the same token it forces an interpretation of *beautiful* in (III') as well. In (13) the opposite forces clash and the sentence explodes. In detail, (13) can be broken down into

She is a dancer who *is* blonde

She is a dancer who *dances* slow*ly*.

Therefore, in view of the different structures involved, the conjunction cannot work, as it cannot work in cases like

    *I took a look at him and an apple.

The selectivity of transformational patterns with respect to the values of their variables permits us to classify adjectives. So I shall affix *1* to those entering (I), *3* to those entering (III′) (and (III) to be given shortly), e.g. red_1, $blond_1$, $fast_3$, $slow_3$, $careful_3$, $beautiful_{13}$, and so on; for variables we will have A_1, A_3, A_{13}, etc. As we go on, I am going to extend this classification.

The relativity I mentioned in connection with A_3's also explains the following transformations:

> He is a slow dancer – His dancing is slow
>
> He is a careful worker – His work is careful.

His dancing and *his work* here are *e*-nominals (see Part One, III,7). This becomes obvious as we select examples like:

> He is a fast polka-dancer – His dancing of the polka is fast
>
> He is a careful chess-player – His playing of chess is careful.

Thus we can generalize as follows:

$$N_i \text{ is } A_3 \ N_V - e \ (N_iV) \text{ is } A_3{}^3$$

and, in case of a transitive verb:

$$N_i \text{ is } A_3 \ N_j \ N_V - e \ (N_i \ V \ N_j) \text{ is } A_3$$

The right sides of these transformations imply, of course, that A_3's are nothing but our familiar Ct_e^A's (Part One, V, 3.). Now with respect to *e*'s, but only with respect to them, A_3's conform to (I):

> slow dance – dance that is slow
>
> careful work – work that is careful;

i.e.:

$$A_3 \ e \leftarrow e \text{ that is } A_3$$

With this in mind, we can suggest an alternative form of (III′), i.e.:

(III′$_a$) $AN_V \leftarrow N_V$ whose e $(V+)$ is A

We can say, therefore, that A_3's are primarily suited for *e*'s and only indirectly for ordinary nouns.[4]

---

[3] $e \ (N_i \ V)$ represents the *e*-nominal product of N_iV. Similarly for $e \ (N_i \ V \ N_j)$ and $e \ (V+)$ in the following formulae (as we recall the subject or the object of the matrix is easily omissible in an *e*).

[4] Here we may speculate about the possibility of viewing all D_{A_3}'s as reduce-able to Ct_e^A's; e.g.:

> He runs fast – His running is fast
>
> He plays tennis well – His playing of tennis is good.

There is another transformation to be mentioned here:

He is a good dancer – He is good at dancing

He is a careful observer – He is careful in observing

i.e.:

N is A_3 N_v – N is A_3 at/in V_{ing}

It is clear that *just* in *just ruler* is an A_3:

just ruler – ruler who rules justly.

If so, then it seems reasonable to assume that *just* functions the same way in *just king* or *just emperor*. Yet, unlike *ruler, king* and *emperor* are not verb-derivatives. Then it is obvious that the co-occurrence of *just* and *king* or *emperor* must determine a verb with respect to which the adjective is ascribed to the noun. This will be, again, *rule* or *govern*. Thus we get the derivation:

just king – king who rules justly.

In general:

$NV + D_{A_3} - e(NV+)$ is A_3.

Looking at things this way, one is tempted to say that D_{A_3} is *like* a predicate attached to a sentence nominalized "by proxy" (See Part One, III, 2, p. 27). As the matrix *He won the race*, in

He won the race, which was unlikely

is regarded as nominalized by virtue of *which*, so *He runs*, in

He runs fast

can be regarded as a quasi-nominal and *fast* as a quasi-predicate. The difference, of course, still remains inasmuch as *unlikely* suggests an *a*- or *d*-nominal, while *fast* an *e*-nominal. Yet even Ct^A_{ad}'s can be forced into the adverbial form:

His arrival is possible – He, possibly, will arrive

That Joe died is probable – Probably, Joe died.

If we add that even a Ct^A_j, like *easy*, is subject to adverbialization (at least through the middle voice) as in

This book is easy to read – This book reads easily

then we realize that *nearly* all adverbs can be related to Ct^A's of various sorts. Even adverbial phrases could be made to conform:

He walks on the street – His walking is on the street

etc. Such a result, of course, would represent an enormous simplification in grammar: adverbs would not appear in elementary sentence-forms. The set of kernel-forms, *NV, NVN, NVNPN*, etc., with the necessary co-occurrence restrictions, and the set of containers again with some co-occurrence restrictions, would be sufficient to derive, by means of the transformations, all sentences of the language. But, obviously, this can only be a tentative suggestion at this stage of research.

We have to resort to the same device to account for a great number of *A N* phrases: *fast horse, slow car, careful scientist, good poet, good father,* and so on. The consideration of this list brings in an additional point: while with respect to *fast horse,* one verb seems to be sufficient, *run,* in the case of *careful scientist* a number of verbs become relevant: *observe, perform experiments, reason, write,* and so forth. What we have to say, therefore, is that in most cases not one verb, but a family of verbs (complete with verb-objects, etc.) is needed to account for the derivation of an A_3N phrase. These verbs are picked out by the co-occurrence of a particular A_3 and N. Not all such co-occurrences are fruitful in this respect. While we understand what a careful scientist or a fast car is, we do not understand (without additional context) what a careful tree or fast apple is.[5]

The concept of an "appropriate" verb-class is applicable at many points in linguistic theory. Take the compound noun: *milkman.* Its analysis can be represented as follows:

$$\text{milkman} - \text{man} \begin{bmatrix} \text{sells} \\ \text{delivers} \\ \text{handles} \\ \text{etc.} \end{bmatrix} \text{milk}$$

Here, again, if the co-occurrence of two nouns fails to pick out relevant verbs, the compound becomes incomprehensible: *milkplanet, fatherman.* The intelligibility of *milkcow, fireman,* on the other hand, is clearly due to the availability of fairly narrow verb-classes.

In these terms, it appears that (III') is nothing but a special case of a much more general transformation, which is

(III) $A \; N \leftarrow N$ wh... $[V+] \; D_A$

with the alternative:

(III$_a$) $A \; N \leftarrow N$ whose $[e \; (V+)]$ is A

While in (III') the appropriate verb is morphologically recoverable

---

[5] The inclination to say, for instance, that a careful mother "mothers" carefully is characteristic: we resort to a clumsy verb to represent a big class.

from the noun, in (III) the verb, or verb-class is merely associated with the noun with respect to the adjective involved.

There are certain nouns that are particularly suited to A_3's and somewhat unsuited to A_1's. Phrases like

>blond king
>tall mother
>big father

are slightly odd. The explanation is that these nouns explicitly denote certain functions (appropriate verb-class), so that we expect A_3's qualifying them with respect to that function. This impression receives support from the fact that exactly these functional nouns can enter the transformation:

>He is a weak king – He is weak as a king
>He is a good father – He is good as a father

i.e.:

>N is A_3 N_f – N is A_3 as N_f

Nouns like *horse, dog, car* are hardly subject to this move. One feels a strain (and a need of explanation) when encountering sentences like

>Nashua is fast as a horse
>Fido is good as a dog
>My Ford is slow as a car

yet *fast horse, good dog, slow car* pass all right. These nouns are only obliquely functional. Therefore, we do not feel any oddity in ascribing A_1's to them:

>fat horse
>big dog
>red car.

Notice that as soon as a function is specified these nouns too can enter the *as*-construction:

>slow as a racehorse
>good as a watchdog.

This construction, in fact, serves to complete "hollow" sentences like

>He is good
>She is slow

where the noun specifying the appropriate verb-class is missing.
So we may add:

>He is good as a poet

>She is slow as a swimmer.

Finally, sentences like

>Our king is weak

>My mother is good

are less natural than, say,

>We have a weak king

>I have a good mother.

The reason is that the copula here is misleading: it suggests (I) while the adjective requires (III). On the contrary, while *blonde mother* is slightly odd

>My mother is blonde

is not odd at all. Here *blonde* is in its natural environment (I), while in *blonde mother*, *mother* suggest (III) which *blonde* cannot enter.

For all these reasons I conclude that the hypothesis of appropriate verb-classes and the given transformation (III) is indeed correct.

3. We have seen that while A_1's are, as it were, transferable from one noun to another, A_3's are not. What I mean is this. Given that all apples are fruits, a red apple has to be a red fruit; similarly a wooden house a wooden building, a hungry cat a hungry animal, and so forth. This generally is not the case with A_3's. All kings are men, but a weak king is not necessarily a weak man; nor is a good mother necessarily a good wife, not to speak of good thieves who are usually bad citizens. The reason by this time is known to us: while A_1's are ascribed to the subject directly, A_3's only with respect to a set of activities (appropriate verb-class) associated with a noun applied to the same subject. This idea of "relative predication" is by no means confined to relativity with respect to verbs or verb-classes. We are going to see that certain adjectives are ascribed to the subject with respect to standard dimensions associated with certain nouns.

The necessity for such a class emerges from the consideration of cases like *small elephant, short python, big flea*. It is clear that these adjectives are not transferable from noun to noun. Although all elephants are animals, a small elephant is not a small animal; although all pythons are snakes, a short python is not a short snake, nor is, a big flea a big insect, in spite of the fact that all fleas are insects. As we recall, the relativity of A_3's could be brought out in the form:

He is good as a thief

He is weak as a king.

In a similar manner, the relativity of "measuring" adjectives can be brought out by the paraphrase:

Jumbo is small for an elephant

Radjah is short for a python.

Another form of the paraphrase would be

Jumbo is small as elephants go.

This gives us the transformation:

(II) A N ← N wh... is A for N

Adjectives conforming to this pattern (A_2's) come in pairs:

big	–	little
large	–	small
long	–	short
thick	–	thin
heavy	–	light
wide	–	narrow

and so on. One side denotes the excess, the other the defect, within a "dimension", with respect to some "standard" associated with a kind. A short python is one that falls short of the standard length of pythons. That these pairs really belong together, can be shown by considering that questions formed in terms of the excess side can be answered in terms of the other:

How long is it? It is short.

How heavy is it? It is light.

There are two other indications as well. The denial of one side leads to the assertion of the other; hence nursery-rhymes to the effect that

What is not large is small

What is not long is short

and so forth. Finally, to say that something is short is to indicate *length*, to say that something is narrow is to indicate *width*, and so on. Notice, however, the asymmetry, in this respect, between excess and defect A_2's. The excess side is "dominant" in an interesting sense. We just mentioned names of dimensions (*length*, *width*), and we could add *height*, *breadth*, that are derived from the name of the excess-side. Again, while the question:

How long is it?

tolerates the answer:

It is short

the question

How short is it?

is not quite properly answered by

It is long.

In other words, while *how long?* has no presupposition about length, *how short?* presupposes shortness (*length* can be *short*, *shortness* cannot be *long*).

Denoting "measure"-nouns, like *size, length, height, width*, etc., by N_m, we can characterize A_2's by the following transformation as well:

(II$_a$) A N ← N whose N_m is A

These features, in addition to the lack of transitivity, mentioned at the beginning of this section, clearly separate A_2's from A_1's. The latter ones (except some special cases to be discussed later) do not come in pairs and the moves we just enumerated cannot be performed on them. One cannot ask how blue is a thing and answer that it is red, and the fact that it is not blue does not entail that it is red. Nor is, say, "redness" the same thing as "color", on the analogy of "length". It is equally easy to prove that A_2's are different from A_3's. The very nature of A_3's requires adverbial derivatives which are essential to (III). A_2's, however, generally do not have adverbial derivatives, and even if they have, the adverb has a remote, often metaphorical, connection with the adjective: *narrowly, hardly, lightly*, etc. At any rate, they are irrelevant to the derivation of A_2 N-phrases, simply because there is no need for verbs there either. What verb, or verb-class, is necessary to the understanding of, say, *short python* or *big flea*? Accordingly, transformations applicable to A_3's fail here. Nothing is big at, or short in doing something, and no doing of a wide road is wide (on the analogy of the good dancing of the good dancer). Many A_3's are indeed contrasting (*fast-slow, good-bad*, etc.), but this by no means proves the identity of transformational structure between A_2N and A_3N phrases.

4. The consideration of phrases like
    easy problem
    difficult language
    comfortable chair
    good soup
    unpleasant climate
makes us realize that they do not fit into any of the patterns thus far discussed. Although it is obvious that these adjectives too are tied to the subject by means of a verb or verb-class, it is equally clear that (III) fails here. Take *easy problem*. The relevant verb is obviously *solve*. An easy problem is one that is easy to solve. Similarly, a difficult language is a language that is difficult to learn, speak, write or understand. Then the difference from (III) becomes clear. In (III) the noun is the subject of the appropriate verb, here the noun is the object: the problem does not solve, but is solved and the language does not learn, but is learnt. Again, while it is the good cook that does the cooking well, it is not the good soup that eats well, the soup is eaten. Thus the key transformation will be:

(IV) A N ← N wh... is A to [V–]

As we see, the subject of the sentence containing the noun as the object of the appropriate verb is not given. Is there any possibility of bringing it in? The answer is in the affirmative:

It is an easy problem *for me* to solve.

In connection with A_3's we mentioned that the appropriate verb can be nominalized and then the adjective can be directly ascribed to the resulting nominal:

(14) John's cooking is slow.

A similar move is possible here too:

(15) The solution of the problem is easy.

Of course, the difference remains: (14) contains a subjective genitive, (15) an objective one. The foregoing points make it abundantly clear that A_4's are nothing but a subclass of Ct_j^A's. Following this hint we can add the transform

It is easy to solve the problem

which, of course, is not available for A_3's. Thus we can collect a battery of transforms suitable for A_4's:

AN$_i$ (for N$_j$ to V—)
N$_i$ wh... is A to V— (for N$_j$)
(for N$_j$) it is A to VN$_i$
t V$_n$ of N$_i$ is A (for N$_j$)

and

(IV$_a$) N$_i$ whose e (V—) is A (for N$_j$)

The remaining Ct_j^A's, like *possible, necessary, superfluous*, and so forth, will fall into different A-classes, since they are applicable to a-nominals, which is not the case with A_4's. Contrast:

It is possible (necessary, etc.) that we solve the problem

*It is easy that we solve the problem.

Since N_i in these forms has to be the object of V, it follows that intransitive verbs are excluded from the class of relevant V's. This, of course, is not true of the V's belonging to A_3's; think of the fast horse that runs fast. The words "verb-object" and "intransitive" have to be taken in a loose sense, however. Take *comfortable chair*. It comes from

chair that is comfortable to sit on

or, in better English,

chair on which one sits comfortably.

This shows that the V— here is *sit on*, and *chair* is the object of this V—.

There are verbs that admit the so-called "middle" transformation either absolutely as, e.g.:

John cooks meat – the meat cooks

or in conjunction with an adverb:

John drives the car easily – the car drives easily

John reads the text easily – the text reads easily.

This might lead to a misunderstanding in connection with A_4's. Take *easy text*; one might say that the source is this:

easy text – text that reads easily

which is like (III), e.g.:

fast horse – horse that runs fast.

The difference, however, becomes clear as soon as we realize that while it is the horse that does the running it is not the text, but the reader, that does the reading.

In connection with A_3N's we remarked that some such combinations are incomprehensible because the pair fails to pick out an appropriate verb-class. Think of *slow table* or *good planet*. A similar situation can occur in the case of A_4N's, for the same reasons. Thus, while *difficult language* or *comfortable chair* are readily understood, *difficult tree* or *easy planet* remain mysterious. Here, however, differently from the case with A_3N's, it is easy to add the relevant verb:

This tree is difficult to grow

Venus is an easy planet to observe.

This device can even overrule the verb-class naturally associated with a particular A_4N. Take *good shoe*. A good shoe, presumably, is good for wearing, walking in, and so on. Yet the Arctic explorer might throw out all this in favor of a verb of his own choice:

This is a good shoe to eat.

This involves *misusing* the shoe. Wearing it, walking in it, and the like, then, is *using* it. Indeed, it is a good intuitive way of characterizing A_4's versus A_3's to say that while A_3's characterize a thing with respect to its functions, A_4's do the same with respect to its use. A perhaps less misleading way of putting this is to say that A_3's are pertinent to what a thing can do or habitually does, but A_4's are pertinent to what can be done or habitually is done with the thing.

The adjective *good*, which is both an A_3 and A_4, has contexts to express this difference very beautifully. If I say

   X is good

one can ask two sorts of questions:

   What is *X* good *at*?
   What is *X* good *for*?

The first question tries to put *good* into (III), the second into (IV).

5. At this point it will be profitable to pause and compile a synopsis of our results. We shall see that the adjectival transformations discussed thus far fall into a coherent and interesting pattern. For the purposes of comparison I shall select the following transformations characterizing the four classes:

   A_1 :   AN – N wh... is A
   A_2 :   AN – N whose N_m is A
   A_3 :   AN – N whose $[e\,(V+)]$ is A
   A_4 :   AN – N whose $[e\,(V-)]$ is A

Then the pattern is clear. While A_1's are directly tied to N by means of the copula, $A_2 - A_4$'s are indirectly tied to N. This "second-hand" connection involves the measure-noun in case of A_2's, and an *e*-nominal in case of $A_3 - A_4$'s with this difference: N is the subject of the *e* with A_3's, and the object of the *e* with A_4's. AN, therefore, in the last three transformations, omits the intervening element, since this element is recoverable given the co-occurrence of a particular A with a particular N. Thus given, say, *big$_2$ stove*, the combination picks out *size* from among the N_m's. Given *fast$_3$ horse*, the co-occurrence suggests *running*; given *easy$_4$ problem*, it offers *solution*.

We have to realize, therefore, that *AN* may be the result of a deletion of redundant elements. This gives us a key to the unraveling of puzzling *AN*'s like

   nuclear scientist
   yellow fever
   infrared lamp

and so forth, where the *N is A* resolution obviously fails. Intuition tells us that the analysis should proceed along the following lines:

nuclear scientist – scientist who [studies] nuclear [phenomena]

yellow fever – fever that [causes] yellow [discoloration]

infrared lamp – lamp that [emits] infrared [rays].

The possibility of this move does not create new adjectival classes. What happens is merely an anticipation of the *A* by an alien *N*, i.e.:

(16) $AN_i - N_i$ wh... [V] A $[N_j]$

Hence the ambiguity in, say, *red lamp* which may mean a lamp which is red or a lamp which emits red light. In the case of *infrared lamp* one path is blocked for semantic reasons. A_3's may show the same kind of alternative. *Good poet* is open to the resolution

poet who writes poems well

which is, of course, straight (III), or to

poet who writes good poems

following the transformation just given. Again, think of the ambiguity in *medieval scholar* as applied to Boethius and E. Gilson.

With respect to many of these cases even (16) is not enough. Take *Wagnerian soprano*. (16) gives:

soprano who [sings] Wagnerian [roles].

Now *Wagnerian role* itself requires an application of (16):

role which [occurs] in Wagnerian [opera].

Thus (16) can be recursively applied, which amounts to the following extension:

(17) $AN_i - N_i$ wh... $[V_i] [N_j]$ wh... $[V_j] [N_k]$ wh...
...wh... $[V_{x-1}] A [N_x]$

Of course, even *Wagnerian opera* requires a transformation:

opera written by Wagner

but this is a different kind of thing, which we will have to investigate later when we shall account for subclasses of A_1's.

There is a small class of adjectives that, at first sight, cannot be accounted for by any of the four schemata we discussed. Some examples of their occurrence:

He is an utter fool
She is a mere child
He is a perfect idiot
It is the bare minimum.

It seems to me that these adjectives are closest to A_3's; they too seem to function in an adverbial role modifying the copulative verb-phrase, *is N*. Indeed, the given examples are transformable into:

He is utterly a fool
She is merely a child
He is perfectly an idiot
It is barely the minimum.

This gives us a transformation analogous to (III):

$$AN \leftarrow N \text{ wh... is } D_A N$$

Furthermore, these adjectives too can be ascribed in some cases to the *e*-nominal of the *N is N* or *N is A* matrix:

his utter stupidity
his sheer idiocy
his mere thoughtlessness.

One can even force a few of them into border-line sentences like

?His stupidity was utter
?His idiocy was perfect.

These forms, of course, try to conform to the (III_a)-pattern.

6.   The small class of adjectives comprising *ready, eager, anxious, willing*, etc. shows a uniform and simple pattern of occurrence:

He is ready to go
He is eager to join the class
He is willing to follow me

and so forth. In spite of the similarity in the *A to V* construction, it is apparent that these adjectives are not A_4's. *V* here is a $V+$ and not a $V-$; the subjects of the two ingredient sentences are identical: *he* is willing and *he* intends to follow me. Accordingly these adjectives do not fit into the battery given in 4. at all. The phrase, however, that we just used, indicates the explanation:

He intends to follow me

is a near paraphrase of

He is willing to follow me.

This reminds us of Ct_h^V's: *want, wish, decide*, etc. Then it becomes clear that the class under consideration, which I shall call A_5's, are nothing but an extension of the class of Ct_h^V's. The possibility of combinations like

He wants to and is ready to go

He has decided to and is eager to join the class

shows this clearly. After all, the very form of *is willing* is a derivative of the verb *will* in the old sense of a Ct_h^V.

A_5's rarely occur in prenominal position. Yet we encounter sentences like

He is an eager man to succeed

He is a willing subject to cooperate.

In view of this possibility I offer:

(V) AN ← N wh... is A to V+

7. The next group to be considered is a numerous and important one. I shall call them A_6's and adjectives like *clever, stupid, reasonable, kind, nice, thoughtful, considerable* and *good* again will belong to the group. Their characteristic occurrence is twofold:

John is stupid to take that job

It is stupid of John to take that job

He was thoughtful to bring flowers

To bring flowers was thoughtful of him.

Thus the adjective is either ascribed to the subject directly with respect to a nominal (*to V+*), or to the nominal directly with respect to the subject. This fact at once indicates the difference from A_5's, which preclude the latter move:

*To join the class was eager of him.

The prenominal position is rare but existent:

John is a stupid man to take that job.

There is a set of additional patterns in which A_6's occur with greater or lesser grammaticality:

John was stupid to have taken that job

Having taken that job was stupid of him

That he took that job was stupid of him.

Although informants hesitate about these forms and purists tend to reject them all, the intuition they reflect is important. As the last examples show, we *feel* that the nominal involved here is more like a *d* than an *e*. This fact suggests an interesting comparison between A_3's and A_6's. As we remember, A_3's are ascribed to an N_i with respect to $e(N_i\ V+)$; here it looks as if we were ascribing the A_6 to an N_i with respect to $d(N_i\ V+)$. Intuitively speaking, while A_3's characterize the doing of a thing (or the subject with respect to the doing), A_6's characterize the thing done (or the subject with respect to it). A_6's indeed refuse the *e*-nominal:

*The taking of that job was stupid of John

*His bringing of flowers was thoughtful.

A_6's can be picked out by using the following battery:

N is A to V+

N is AN to V+

to V+ is A of N (it is A of N to V+)

This last form demonstrates that A_6's are identical with the class of Ct_K's (Part One, IV, 6). There are two added forms of dubious grammaticality:

V_{ing} + is A of N

that NV+ is A of N (it is A of N that NV+)[6]

8. We recall (from 4.) that a group of Ct_j^A's had to be separated from A_4's because they enter the frame:

(18) that NV+ is A (it is A that NV+)

---

[6] A_6's, like A_3's, have adverbial derivatives. But notice the difference:

    John walks slowly

    John, stupidly, took that job at once.

The pauses in the second sentence indicate that *stupidly* is more aloof than *slowly* in the previous sentence. And no wonder, since *slow* needs only a nominalized verb to apply (*slow walk*), but *stupid* has to nominalize the whole sentence (since *stupid taking (of) that job at once* will not do). If I may say so, while *slowly* is a verb-adverb, *stupidly* is a sentence adverb. Notice the different roles of the two adverbs, *stupidly* and *at once*, in the last example.

which is barred to A_4's like *easy* or *difficult*. The group thus emerging contains *possible, necessary, profitable,* etc., and their opposites. It is obvious that although they enter the A_4-battery, they show a still greater affinity to another group mainly characterized by (18), which, however, does not fit into the A_4-battery. This last group contains *probable, certain, likely, true* and their opposites. Since even this last group shows a cleavage, the best we can do at this point is to set up a wide sample of schemata and test the adjectives involved as to their affinities in order to arrive at some classification. I suggest the following collection:

(19) N_j wh... is A to V – (for N_i)
(20)   (for N) it is A to V$+$
(21) e (V$+$) is A (for N)
(22) d (NV$+$) is A
(23) d (N_iV$+$) is A for N_j
(24) a (NV$+$) is A
(25) a (N_iV$+$) is A for N_j

For easier comprehension I illustrate these schemata using the matrix *He runs the race.* Thus we get:

(19a)   ... race which is *A* to run (for him)
(20a)   (For him) it is *A* to run the race
(21a)   The running of the race is *A* (for him)
(22a)   His running the race is *A*
(23a)   His running the race is *A* for me
(24a)   That he runs the race is *A*
(25a)   That he runs the race is *A* for me.

Now, *easy, difficult, pleasant* and *unpleasant* enter (19), (20), (21) and refuse the rest. They, therefore, are pure A_4's.

Possible and *impossible* enter all forms except (23) and (25). I shall call them A_7's.

Useful, profitable, necessary, and their opposites enter all forms. These will be A_8's.

Probable, likely, certain and their opposites enter (22) and (24) and refuse the rest. They will be A_9's.

True and *false* enter only (24) and refuse the rest.[7]

The significance of this sequence can be understood as follows. While A_3's and A_4's correspond to *e*-nominals, $A_7 - A_9$'s apply to *a – d*-nominals. Since *e*-nominals are easily separable from the object or the subject of the matrix, it is not surprising that A_3's and A_4's can easily enter into an *AN*-construction following the transformation:

AN – N whose *e* (V$\pm$) is A

a – d-nominals, on the other hand, are results of nominalizations *in indivisibili* (Part One, III, 6), consequently, as we move from A_7's to A_9's the adjective shows less and less inclination to get attached to a noun in the matrix. Although we accept sentences like

(26) This is an impossible plan to follow
(27) It is a useful book to read
(28) He is an unlikely man to succeed

this pattern is quite shaky, as the following counterexamples show:

*This is a possible problem to solve

*This is an unnecessary tree to cut

*Eucalyptus is an improbable tree to grow in our climate.

Incidentally, if this move is possible, then A_7's and A_8's get attached to the object of the matrix (see (26)-(27)) while A_9's to the subject (see (28)). This corresponds to the affinity between A_4's, A_7's and A_8's. After all, they share the A_4-battery in common.

This last fact does not contradict our claim that A_7's and A_8's are not *e*-containers, while A_4's are. We recall that *d*-containers are tolerant to receive morphological *e*'s. The possibility of the *a*-paraphrase clarifies the issue. Compare:

(29) The solution of the problem is difficult (for us)
(30) The solution of the problem is impossible (for us).

[7] They can be forced into (22), as in
     His writing novels these days is true
     His being innocent is false.
For this reason, and for the smallness of the class, I shall not separate them from the other A_9's.

Obviously only (30) is transformable into the *a*-form
> It is impossible that we (can) solve the problem
> *It is difficult that we solve the problem.

Moreover, while (29) tolerates the addition of a Ct_e^N, (30) does not:
> The solution of the problem is a difficult process
> *The solution of the problem is an impossible process.

9. I claim that the classification of adjectives just given is complete. In this concluding section I intend to show that I have distinguished all *possible* major adjectival classes. This proof is feasible as, in view of Part One, we have a clear command of the kinds of noun-phrase to which adjectives can apply. It is obvious that from the point of view of adjectives the relevant classes are the following: original nouns, *e*-nominals and *a-d*-nominals. We noticed in addition that adjectives that are suited to nominals can also be applied to a noun-element (subject or object) of the nominal, with respect to the remainder of the nominal, or to the incomplete nominal, with respect to the missing noun-element. In such cases the cut-off parts are brought in by means of a characteristic preposition. These considerations provide the following abstract possibilities:

(31) N is A
(32) e (N$_i$ V N$_j$) is A
(33) N$_i$ is A P inc. e (V N$_j$)
(34) inc. e (V N$_j$) is A P N$_i$
(35) N$_j$ is A P inc. e (N$_i$ V—)
(36) inc. e (N$_i$ V—) is A P N$_j$
(37) $a - d$ (N$_i$ V N$_j$) is A
(38) N$_i$ is A P inc. $a - d$ (V N$_j$)
(39) inc. $a - d$ (V N$_j$) is A P N$_i$
(40) N$_j$ is A P inc. $a - d$ (N$_i$ V—)
(41) inc. $a - d$ (N$_i$ V—) is A P N$_j$

For easier comprehension I illustrate these possibilities:

(31a) The rose is *A*
(32a) His running of the race is *A*

(33a)   He is *A in* running the race
(34a)   To run the race is *A for* him
(35a)   The race is *A for* him to run
(36a)   vacuous
(37a)   His running the race is *A*
(38a)   He is *A to* run the race
(39a)   To run the race is *A of/for* him
(40a)   The race is *A for* him to run
(41a)   vacuous.

Then it is clear that the following correspondences hold:

A_1 :   (31)
A_3 :   (32), (33)
A_4 :   (34), (35)
A_5 :   (38)
A_6 :   (38), (39)
A_7 :   (37), (39), (40)
A_9 :   (37)

The result is not as neat as one could wish. There is some overlap among the higher-order adjectives, there is the *of/for* difference in (39a), (*stupid of him, possible for him*) and there is no place for A_2's and A_8's. The previous text supplies the deficiencies of this synopsis however. As it is, the transformational behavior of English adjectives can be brought into an obvious correlation with our findings on nominalizations.

VII. PREDICATE ADJECTIVES: *N wh... is A.* (A_1)

1. The class of A_1's is a grab-bag of adjectives. All color- and shape-words seem to belong to it, then the adjectives denoting kinds, nationalities, religions and what not, all present and past participles and some other verb derivatives, finally some more or less contrastive adjectives like *warm, cold, beautiful, ugly, gay, sad, young, old* and so forth.

The main reason for grouping them together is their noun-neutrality, i.e., the possibility of transfer from noun to noun in the sense mentioned in Chapter VI, 3. As we know, a short python is not a short snake, and a good thief may be a bad man. A gray or angry or carnivorous python, on the other hand, is a gray or angry or carnivorous snake. Similarly, a German physicist is a German scientist, a German man and, if he is a chess-player, a German chess-player, and so on. True, he can become, say, a French soldier, but then *French soldier* is not taken in the sense of (I), i.e.:

French soldier – soldier who is French

but rather in the sense of the "nuclear scientist" transformation (see (16) in the previous chapter), that is:

French soldier – soldier who [serves in] French [army].

It is due to this noun-neutrality that (I) adequately characterizes A_1's. The adjective is absolutely ascribed to the subject, not with respect to a specific noun- or verb-class. Hence the following transformation will be truth-preserving:

N_i is A_1 N_j – N_j is A_1 N_i

For instance:

This man is a German scientist – This scientist is a German man

This animal is a carnivorous mammal – This mammal is a carnivorous animal

My car is a red Ford – My Ford is a red car.

With respect to some contrastive A_1's (*warm, cold*, and so on) this move might fail, but, as we shall see, this class forms a bridge to A_2's. Finally, the same noun-neutrality explains the impossibility of fitting A_1's into transforms characterizing other classes: *He is German as a scientist, *He is German to V—.

This does not mean that the same adjectives cannot belong to more than one class. We have seen examples of such adjectives: *beautiful*$_{13}$, *good*$_{3468}$. The point is that the classes themselves remain distinct.

There are many criteria that can be followed in establishing subclasses of A_1's. Morphological derivation (suffixes turning nouns or verbs into adjectives: *dolomitic, silky, catlike, broken, active*), possibility of occurring as a noun (*yellow, German,* but not *dolomitic, sad, angular*), possibility of having an adverbial derivative (*radical, awful,* but not *red, Italian*), semantic classes (color-words, shape-words, "emotive" words: *horrible, lovely*), etc. The method I shall follow will be primarily transformational: with respect to derived adjectives, I shall determine the transformation that turns a noun or a verb into an adjective. In doing so we will be guided by the suffixes, assuming that identity of suffixes probably indicates identity of derivation. At this point we face a problem. It happens that verbs and nouns of Latin origin tend to keep Latin suffixes (the same holds with respect to a few Greek ones too). The result is that we have parallel Germanic and Latin suffixes corresponding to the same derivation. The picture is complicated by the fact that the original Latin noun may be missing from English. I give a few illustrations: *catlike* is *cat* + *like*. The corresponding *feline* is from the Latin *felinus*, which is *felis* + *inus*. But *felis* does not exist in English. Again, take *fatal* and *mortal* from the Latin *fatalis* and *mortalis*.

Now *fatum* has an English version: *fate*. *Mors*, on the other hand, does not have an English noun-form. I shall regard *feline* and *mortal* as noun-derivatives, notwithstanding the fact that there is no *mors* or *felis* in English. Similarly with verbs: *readable* affixes a suffix of Latin origin (*ble* from *bilis*) to an English verb (*read*). Now *legible* does the same thing to a Latin root which has no verb-equivalent in English. Yet I shall take *legible* as a verb-derivative nevertheless. After having dealt with derived A_1's I shall complete the classification by considering original ones as well (like *red, sad*, etc.).

2. I begin with noun-derivatives. In surveying the various suffixes (and the corresponding derivations) I shall pay particular attention to the existence or non-existence of adverbial forms. If there is no adverbial form, then I shall assume that the adjective primarily applies to straight nouns and only secondarily to nominalized verbs (e (V)); if there is an adverbial form, then I take the reverse to be the case. Take *Russian* versus *radical*, and *politician* versus *move*. Now a Russian politician is a politician who is from Russia. A Russian move on the other hand is not a move that is from Russia, but a move made by some people who are from Russia. A radical move, on the other hand, is a move that goes to the root of the matter (*radix*), while a radical politician is one whose actions go to the root of the matter. This corresponds to the fact that we can act radically but not Russianly.

A_a:

$N(\text{zero})$: iron bar, ice crystal, silk stocking

N_{en} : wooden box, silken scarf, brazen pot.

The nouns are mass-nouns. Adjectives specify the material of the thing. The source is this:

$$N_{en}\ N_i \leftarrow N_i\ wh... \begin{bmatrix} \text{consists of} \\ \text{is made of} \\ \text{etc.} \end{bmatrix} N$$

Or we can use the word "material":

$N_{en} \; N_i \leftarrow N_i$ whose material is N

Or, simply,

$N_{en} \; N_i \leftarrow N_i$ wh... is (of) N

No adverbial (except metaphorical, like *woodenly, brazenly*).

A_b:

N_{ic}	:	epidermic cancer, metallic surface, Punic war
N_{an}	:	Bolivian ore, Wagnerian opera, human hand
N_{ine}	:	canine tooth, feline mammal, leonine face
N_{ese}	:	Portuguese ship, Japanese silk, Maltese cross
N_{ish}	:	Turkish coffee, Polish logician, Scottish town, snobbish manners, clannish attitude
N_{al}	:	tonal music, theatrical effect.

The derivation of these phrases is manifold. There are three "standard" derivations and several specific ones. The first kind of standard derivation is exemplified in the following:

epidermic cancer	–	cancer on the epidermis
Punic war	–	war against Puns
Bolivian ore	–	ore from Bolivia
Wagnerian opera	–	opera by Wagner
human hand	–	hand of man
canine tooth	–	tooth of dog
Scottish town	–	town in Scotland
tonal music	–	music in tones:

In general:

(α) $N_{ic} \; N_i \leftarrow N_i$ wh...is P N

I do not inquire into the remote origins of the *N P N*-phrase. In most cases we could recover a "lost" verb; e.g.:

Punic war	–	war [fought] against Puns
Wagnerian opera	–	opera [written] by Wagner.

Some of the adjectives thus derived occur as nouns as well:

Bolivian man	–	a Bolivian
Portuguese woman	–	a Portuguese

etc. This is restricted to adjectives ascribed to "human" words (man, woman, child, etc.). The adjectives themselves come from geographical nouns (Bolivia, Portugal). Notice that N_{ish} and N_{ic} are exempt from this rule, because N here is not a name of a country, but the name of a nationality (*Pun, Turk*). So we don't have **a Turkish*, or **a Punic*.

The second standard derivation is this:

metallic stuff	–	stuff like metal
feline mammal	–	mammal like cat
greenish color	–	color like green

i.e.:

(β) N_{ic} N_i ← N_i wh...is like N

In case of $N_i = $ *being, animal,* etc., N_{an} and N_{ine} occur as nouns:

human being	–	a human
feline animal	–	a feline.

The third derivation is a combination of (α) and (β):

metallic surface	–	surface like that of metal
leonine face	–	face like that of lion
Wagnerian style	–	style like that of Wagner
Irish face	–	face like that of an Irishman

i.e.:

(γ) N_{ic} N_i ← N_i wh... is like that of N

In addition, there are many individual derivations, like

Maltese cross – cross like the ones used by knights from Malta

Turkish coffee – coffee like that brewed by Turks.

Similar complicated and unique derivation is required for phrases like *Chinese checkers, Polish notation* (in logic), *Greek gift, Basque hat*, and so on. These phrases are, as it were, petrified; they cannot be broken up. Compare:

Maltese wooden cross

wooden Maltese cross.

The first is a wooden cross from Malta. The second is a wooden cross that looks like etc. Similarly,

woolen Basque hat
Basque woolen hat

and so forth. We have to conclude that the source of A_bN phrases cannot be determined without considering N as well as A_b.

Some, but not all, N's forms can be regarded as adjectives; e.g.: *expensive children's shoes, women's silk underwear, fine violinist's hand,* and so on. They generally conform to (α) and (γ) above.

children's shoe – shoe for children (α)
violinist's hand – hand like that of a violinist (γ).

Thus, they can be regarded as A_b's too. This is confirmed by the fact that their place in a prenominal string is between A_a's and A_c's: *silky$_c$ women's underwear, women's silk$_a$ underwear* (see Chapter VIII.). N, moreover, can take adjectives in this position too; hence the ambiguity in *small children's shoes,* which may come from

small shoes for children

or

shoes for small children.

Other N's forms are not adjectival, but indicate another noun-phrase: *John's shoes, The children's small shoes,* and so on. They split as follows:

the shoes of John
the small shoes of the children.

Thus both N's in the N's N form can take the definite article (except in case of proper names). This is not true of the previous kind. *Expensive children's shoes* does not go into

expensive shoes for the children.

Unfortunately, some N's N phrases remain ambiguous in this respect; *these children's shoes* has two derivations:

the shoes of these children
these shoes for children.

Ambiguities can be combined; *these small children's shoes* has three obvious derivations:

these shoes for small children
these small shoes for children
the shoes of these small children.

Further details would require a complete treatment of noun-phrases, which is beyond the scope of the present paper.

A_c:

N_{like} : catlike mamal, steellike substance, childlike face
N_y : silky material, bushy tail, fluffy cake.

These adjectives are like the previous except that (α) does not apply to them. (β) and (γ) do:

(β) catlike mammal   – mammal like cat
   steellike substance – substance like steel
   silky material   – material like silk
   bushy tail   – tail like bush
(γ) childlike face   – face like that of child
   catlike eye   – eye like that of cat
   silky texture   – texture like that of silk
   brassy voice   – voice like (sound) of brass.

No noun occurrences and no adverbials.

A_d:

N_{al} : radical step, mortal wound, dorsal fin
N_{ical} : logical process, tyrannical rule, political life.

The first thing to remark here is the possibility of adverbial derivation. Consider *historic* and *historical*; only the second takes *-ly*. This indicates that A_d's are primarily suited to nominalized verbs. Indeed, most of our examples contain such. Even *dorsal fin* can be analyzed *fin that has dorsal position*. Some derivations:

radical step   – step going to the root (of the matter)
mortal wound   – wound causing death
logical process   – process according to logic

and for adverbial forms:

radically   – going to the root (of the matter)
orally   – done through the mouth
verbally   – done in words

and so forth. Thus I suggest:

$N_{al} \, e \, (V) \leftarrow e \, (V) \, wh... \, [V \, P] \, N$

or simply

N_{a1} e (V) ← e (V) wh... is P N.

If A_d is attributed to straight nouns (*radical politician, mortal weapon, dorsal fin*), then I postulate the existence of a deleted but recoverable *nom* (V), and give the transformation:

N_{a1} N_i ← N_i whose e (V) [V P] N

or

N_{a1} N_i ← N_i whose e (V) is P N

A_e:

N_{ish} :   foolish action, childish talk, impish smile:

This group is similar to the previous. Again, there are adverbials; thus I assume that A_e's apply primarily to verb-nominals. The derivation is somewhat different:

foolish action   –   action that is like that of a fool
childish talk   –   talk that is like that of a child

thus

N_{ish} e (V) ← e (V) wh... is like that of N

If applied to straight nouns, like *foolish girl, childish man*, then I make the move I made above, i.e.:

N_{ish} N_i ← N_i whose [e (V)] is like that of N

A_g:

N_{ar} :   rectangular window, granular stone, lunar orbit.

N usually denotes some geometrical feature (shape, texture, direction, etc.). Thus I suggest:

$$N_{ar}\ N_i \leftarrow N_i \text{ whose } \begin{bmatrix} \text{shape} \\ \text{texture} \\ \text{etc.} \end{bmatrix} \text{[V] N}$$

So it seems that N_{ar} is directly attributed to an abstract noun (*shape, texture, orbit, location*, etc.) and only through this to a concrete noun. Accordingly, we can give the source in two steps:

$$N_{ar}\ N_i \leftarrow N_i \text{ wh... has } N_{ar} \begin{bmatrix} \text{shape} \\ \text{texture} \\ \text{etc.} \end{bmatrix}$$

and

$$N_{ar} \begin{bmatrix} \text{shape} \\ \text{texture} \\ \text{etc.} \end{bmatrix} \leftarrow \begin{bmatrix} \text{shape} \\ \text{texture} \\ \text{etc.} \end{bmatrix} \text{wh... [V] N}$$

Later we will see that this line of derivation applies to some other shape-words too.

A_h:

N_{ous}	:	luminous star, gaseous medium, humorous story
N_{ose}	:	otiose move, verbose report, porous stone
N_{ful}	:	colorful room, beautiful picture, powerful fist
N_{less}	:	colorless room, shapeless rock, bottomless pit
N_y	:	dirty cloth, filthy hole, greasy soup.

Individual analysis:

luminous star	–	star that emits plenty of light
verbose report	–	report that contains plenty of words
powerful fist	–	fist that has plenty of power
shapeless rock	–	rock that has no shape
dirty cloth	–	cloth that has plenty of dirt.

Generally:

$$N_{ous} \ N_i \leftarrow N_i \ \text{wh...} \begin{bmatrix} \text{has} \\ \text{contains} \\ \text{etc.} \end{bmatrix} Q \ N$$

where Q is *plenty of, no, little*, etc.

Some of the A_h's have adverbials, others not. Here the difference does not seem to be important.

3. So much about noun-derivatives. Now I compile the list of verb-derivatives.

A_i:

V_{ing}	:	floating ice, sleeping girl, moving scene
V_{nt}	:	resilient spring, vacant house, dormant volcano.

These are English and Latin present paticiples. The source is clear:

$$V_{ing} \ N_i \leftarrow N_i \ \text{wh...} \ V+$$

A_j:

V_{en}	:	broken pot, grown tree, aged wine
V_t	:	defunct species, inept person, abrupt move.

These are past participles. Thus:

$$V_{en} \ N_i \leftarrow N_i \ wh... \ is \ V_{en} - (by \ N_j)$$

Thus the derivation goes through the passive or short passive.

A_k:

V_{ive}	:	active volcano, passive resistence, impulsive person
V_{id}	:	rabid dog, morbid person, tepid water
V_y	:	shiny coin, glittery crystal, racy story
V_{und}	:	moribund person
V_{urn}	:	taciturn person.

Here the verb comes in *via* some modality indicating inclination, proneness, likelihood:

$$V_{ive} \ N_i \leftarrow N_i \ wh... \ [mod] \ V+$$

A_l:

V_{ble}	:	breakable glass, soluble salt, readable book
V_{ile}	:	fragile glass, mobile home, docile child.

Source as above, but through the passive:

$$V_{ble} \ N_i \leftarrow N_i \ wh... \ [mod] \ be \ V_{en} - (by \ N_j)$$

A_x:

$nom(V)_{ful}$	:	dreadful face, awful story, frightful load
$nom(V)_{ble}$	:	horrible face, terrible event, abominable monster

These are "emotive" adjectives. They attribute to the subject an emotional reaction evoked in a human (dread, horror, fright, delight, awe, etc.). Source:

$$e\,(V)_{ful} \ N_i \leftarrow N_i \ wh... \begin{bmatrix} evokes \\ causes \\ etc. \end{bmatrix} e\,(V) \ in \ N_j$$

In some cases the following works too:

$$e(V)_{ful} \ N_i \leftarrow N_i \ wh... \ V_{fies} \ N_j$$

e.g.:

terrible event	–	event that terrifies N
horrible end	–	end that horrifies N

(hence we even have *terrific*). These, of course, come from *terrorem, horrorem facere*.

There is a peculiar occurrence of emotive adjectives. They can occur as one-word exclamations expressing emotional reaction:

(How) terrible!

(How) dreadful!

It is obvious that most members of the A_x class, and some of the previous classes (like *stupid*), occur as adjectives of higher classes (A_{6-3}) as well. *Beautiful*, incidentally, sometimes has the force of an A_x:

(How) beautiful!

The same about *lovely, pretty, etc.*

4.   Having enumerated the most common forms of derived A_1's, it is time to turn to the underived ones. They seem to fall into two main classes: color-words (with a few original shape-words thrown in) and more or less contrastive adjectives, like *warm, hot, cold, gay, sad, young, old, fat, lean.*

I mentioned that original shape-words conform to the pattern of A_g's (*rectangular*, etc.). Indeed, with respect to *round, square,* or even such derived ones as *oval*, the transformations

A N_i – N_i whose shape is A

A N_i – N_i wh... has A shape

A N_i –   the shape of N_i is A

will hold. Therefore, I shall put all shape-words, regardless of their form, into the class: A_g.

Then we realize that all color-words, original ones, like *red, yellow, green, blue, white, black, gray,* and derived ones, like *orange, purple, magenta, pink, rose, garnet,* etc., conform to similar transformations, that is:

A N_i – N_i whose color is A

A N_i – N_i wh... has A color

A N_i –   the color of N_i is A

Here we even have:

A is a color

while the corresponding

A is a shape

sounds less good.

Consequently, I shall put all color-words, regardless of their form, into a category neighboring A_g: A_f.

Finally, I shall assign all contrasting, or more or less contrasting. A_1's to the class A_m. It is clear that this class is a bridge between A_1's and A_2's. Certain A_2 forms work for some A_m's, but not all for all. An old man is not old for a man, a sad face is not sad for a face. Warm ice, on the other hand, can be said to be warm as ice goes. Again, while the questions and answers:

> How old is he? He is young.
> How warm is it? It is cold.

are fully acceptable,

> How gay is he? He is sad.

is not quite the same.

Similarly, while age and temperature can be called, in a sense, dimensions (admit measure), moods do not.

5. By way of a summary, I reproduce the characteristic transformations for each of the derived subclasses of A_1's:

A_a	:	$N_{en} N_i$	— N_i wh... is (of) N
A_b	:	$N_{ic} N_i$	— N_i wh... is P N
			wh... is like N
			wh... is like that of N
A_c	:	$N_{like} N_i$	— N_i wh... is like N
			wh... is like that of N
A_d	:	$N_{al}e$ (V)	— e(V) wh... [V P] N
A_e	:	$N_{ish}e$ (V)	— e(V) wh... is like that of N
A_f	:	A N	— N whose color is A
A_g	:	$N_{ar} N_i$	— N_i whose [shape] [V] N
A_h	:	$N_{ous} N_i$	— N_i wh... [has] Q N
A_i	:	$V_{ing} N_i$	— N_i wh... V+
A_j	:	$V_{en} N_i$	— N_i wh... is V_{en} – (by N_j)
A_k	:	$V_{ive} N_i$	— N_i wh... [mod] V+
A_l	:	$V_{ble} N_i$	— N_i wh... [mod] be V_{en} – (by N_j)
A_x	:	e(V)$_{ful} N_i$	— N_i wh... [V] e(V) in N_j

The more or less contrastive A_m's complete the division.

VIII. ORDER OF ADJECTIVES

1. Nouns may take more than one adjective at a time. This can occur in three regular ways:

(1) My house is big and beautiful

(2) That is a big and beautiful house

(3) That is a big beautiful house.

There is a fourth, somewhat rhetorical version:

(4) I have a house, big and beautiful.

(1), (2) and, when desired, (4) can be handled together. The variations:

N is A_y C A_z

A_y C A_z N

N, A_y C A_z

hold or fail together. Such combinations are not restricted to two adjectives. Three, or even more, can be combined:

long, narrow but straight road

and so forth. There are restrictions, however, as to the quality of the adjectives that can be thus combined:

*long and Polish word

*wooden and comfortable chair

*green and broken vase

etc. are ruled out. There is another, less cogent restriction:

red and yellow flowers

long and narrow road

sound better than

yellow and red flowers

narrow and long road.

The constraints affecting forms like (3) are more strict and important. It is easy to produce $A\ A \ldots A\ N$ strings that require a more or less definite order of succession:

> big beautiful white wooden house
> comfortable red chair
> big rectangular green Chinese silk carpet.

Combinations like

> *white wooden beautiful big house
> *red comfortable chair
> *Chinese big silk green rectangular carpet

are felt as peculiar or even ungrammatical.

In this section I shall be concerned with the restrictions affecting the "broken" forms, i.e., (1), (2), and (4). The much more formidable problems besetting the unbroken strings, like (3), will be left for the next section.

I begin by disposing of a side issue. As we saw we prefer

> red and yellow
> long and narrow

to

> yellow and red
> narrow and long.

Here we are influenced by a simple phonetic rule: in joining words by *and* or *or*, the shorter element comes first:

> black and white
> up and down
> in and out
> fields and meadows
> odds and ends
> nuts and bolts

and so on. This simple rule, once recognized, orders all otherwise permissible *A and A*, *A or A* cases. *A but* (*yet, etc.*) *A* may have other considerations overruling phonetic aspects. About this later.

Having thus disposed of the minor issue, we are ready to examine the restrictions affecting the co-occurrence of adjectives themselves. We shall see that they depend, in part at least, on the connective particle. *Or* seems to have the strictest requirements, *and* somewhat less strict ones, *but, yet, nevertheless* very loose ones. To begin with, I shall take *and* for a paradigm.

First I recall the example I used in Chapter VI, 2:

*She is a blonde and fast dancer:

This fails, because one deleted part of the ingredient sentence:

She *dances* fast

is not to be found in the other ingredient:

She is blonde.

Contrast this with the acceptable:

She is tall and blonde

where the same copula connects both adjectives to the same subject. This, of course, is but a particular application of a general rule governing all sorts of conjunctive deletions. It is roughly as follows:

$$S(X\ Y)\ C\ S(X\ Z) - S(X\ Y\ C\ Z)$$

i.e.: one occurrence of the identical element, X, gets zeroed and the disparate ones conjoined. Thus, ideally, any $A\ C\ A$ string presupposes the identity of the remaining elements in the ingredient sentences including the way the A's are tied to the subject. Moreover, the failure of conjunctions like

*He saw red and an apple

*He took a look at him and a piece of cake

convinces us that the identity thus presupposed is not merely a morphological one, but involves transformational sources as well. Therefore, although

She is a fast dancer

She is a blonde dancer

are morphologically identical except for the two adjectives, the difference in transformational source prevents the conjunction. For the same reason

*long and Polish word

fails, since *long* is tied to *word* by (II) (see VI, 3), while *Polish* is brought in either by (α) of A_b's (see VII, 2.):

word [used] by Poles

or, even more likely, by an "unorthodox" transformation (like *Maltese Cross*), i.e.:

    word belonging to language used by Poles.

Similarly, for instance,

    *green and comfortable chair

tries to combine an A_f with an A_4. "Ideal" combinations, there-fore, will remain in the same category:

    copper$_a$ and iron$_a$ tools
    human$_a$ and canine$_b$ bones
    Oriental$_b$ and domestic$_b$ blends
    red$_f$ and white$_f$ stripes
    running$_i$ and turbulent$_i$ water
    broken$_j$ and shattered$_j$ remains
    passive$_k$ and taciturn$_k$ people
    long$_2$ and narrow$_2$ road
    fast$_3$ and lively$_3$ dancer
    thoughtful$_6$ and considerate$_6$ husband
    unlikely$_9$ and uncertain$_9$ conclusion

I do not enter here into considerations of incompatibility and of ambiguities in sentences like

    I see red and green houses

which obviously may come from either

    I see houses that are red
    I see houses that are green

or

    I see houses that are red and green.

There are acceptable derivations from the "ideal". *And*, as we said, is more tolerant than *or* in this respect. Phrases like

    old$_m$ and broken$_j$ pot
    big$_2$ and beautiful$_h$ house
    large$_2$ and comfortable$_4$ chair
    clever$_6$ and profitable$_8$ venture

are tolerable. But we cannot push this too far:

    ? big$_2$ and round$_g$ hole
    ? deep$_2$ and black$_f$ hole
    ? round$_g$ and yellow$_f$ patch

are questionable.

    *Fast$_3$ and yellow$_f$ car
    *tall$_2$ and slow$_3$ dancer
    *long$_2$ and false$_9$ statement
    *green$_f$ and running$_i$ water
    *red$_f$ and broken$_j$ vase
    *thick$_2$ and dolomitic$_b$ formation

etc., are clearly wrong. Now *or* is much more exacting: it truly requires alternatives within the same category. Thus while

    iron$_a$ or copper$_a$ tools
    volcanic$_b$ or sedimentary$_b$ rocks
    pink$_f$ or red$_f$ flowers
    round$_g$ or oval$_g$ grains
    active$_k$ or dormant$_k$ volcano
    long$_2$ or short$_2$ dresses
    clever$_6$ or stupid$_6$ move
    true$_8$ or false$_8$ statement

can occur,

    *new$_m$ or broken$_j$ pots
    *small$_2$ or comfortable$_4$ chair
    *big$_2$ or round$_g$ hole

cannot. Moreover, even within the same category, like A_2, *or* requires the same aspect, e.g., the same dimension. Thus while

    long or short

is acceptable,

    *long or thin

is not.

As we move to *but, yet,* and *nevertheless,* we find much greater freedom:

    dolomitic$_b$ but dark$_m$ rock
    new$_m$ but broken$_j$ pen
    metallic$_b$ yet soft$_m$ material.

In postnominal position even

    She is Italian$_b$ but tall$_2$
    The furniture is steel$_a$ yet comfortable$_4$

might be accepted. Here, of course, another restriction enters the picture. While

    thin but strong rope

    small but heavy stone

are all right,

    ? thick but strong rope

    ? big but heavy stone

are not. The reason is obvious: these connectives indicate contrasts and since we expect thick ropes to be strong and big stones to be heavy, there is no contrast here. The same way as

    She is Swedish but tall

would be odd. But this is a semantical matter. Incidentally, as

    Swedish but short

shows, the above mentioned phonetic rule is discarded here: *Swedish* is longer than *short* yet it comes first. The reason is that while *and* and *or* are usually symmetrical, *but*, etc., need not be. In our case the relevant inference goes from *Swedish* to *tall* not from *tall* to *Swedish*. And exactly that inference is contrasted by *short*.

2.   Finally, we are ready to deal with the problem that originally motivated this whole study, the one concerning the natural order of adjectives in unbroken prenominal strings. The almost complete solution of this problem will provide a reason for thinking that our results thus far are essentially correct.

As I said in the previous section, most strings of this kind require a specific order of succession among the members. Examples like

    beautiful white wooden house

    comfortable red chair

    big rectangular green Chinese carpet

are sufficient to illustrate the point: hardly any change in the order is possible. What, then, are the principles determining the order?

To begin with, I contrast, once more, broken and unbroken sequences. We saw that broken constructions like

    *long and Polish word

    *wooden and comfortable chair

*green and broken vase

are not acceptable because the adjectives involved have different transformational nexus to the subject. This shows, indirectly, that the adjectives in a correct sequence of this kind, like

long and narrow road

are brought in by the same operation (let it be called Ω_i):

$\Omega_i (A_z C A_y) N$

In other words, the adjectives here are *coordinated*. Unbroken sequences, on the other hand, easily incorporate adjectives requiring different operations. The same groups form the perfectly acceptable

long Polish word

comfortable wooden chair

broken green vase.

Accordingly, what we have here must be a case of *subordination*, i.e.:

$\Omega_i (A_z) [\Omega_j (A_y) [\Omega_k (A_w) [...[\Omega_l (A_v) N]] ...]$

More explicitly, while the genealogy of the broken string is this:

$N \ wh... \ \Omega_i (A_z C A_y)$

that of an unbroken one is rather like this:

$[[[... [N \ wh... \ \Omega_i A_v] ...] \ wh... \ \Omega_j A_y] \ wh... \ \Omega_l A_z]$

In terms of a simpler symbolism, the two ways are contrasted as

$(A C A) N$

$A [A [...[AN]] ...]$

It can be expected, therefore, that the natural order of adjectives be a function of the transformational operations appropriate to the various kinds of adjective. This, of course, implies that these operations are applied in a definite order. Now my claim is that the order of their application is the order stipulated by the classification of adjectives given in this paper from A_1 to A_9, and within A_1 from A_a to A_x. Given a noun N and two adjectives A_z and A_y, such that z is higher than y in the given sense, first A_y will be joined to N, giving

A_y N

then A_z will be joined to this compound

A_z A_y N

The same, with obvious extensions, for phrases involving more than two adjectives. The ideal, but never obtainable, noun-phrase will be then

A_9 A_8 ... A_2 A_x A_m ... A_a N

That such a monster is not produceable is due to the fact that certain classes of adjectives are suited only to nominalized sentences, others to nominalized verbs, others to nouns. Thus a thing like *probable* will hardly apply to a thing to which *red* or *dolomitic* applies. Of course they might occasionally go together in contexts like

... of probable dolomitic structure.

The rule holds anyway.

The real test of the hypothesis should be sought in the innumerable varieties of adjectival strings affixed to regular nouns. These, naturally, will consist of the various sorts of A_1, then A_2, (sometimes) A_3, and A_4. Thus, I submit a small selection, which shows that our theory accounts for all conceivable kinds of prenominal string. Informants might argue that the order in some of these cases is not *that* strict. This is quite possible. Later I shall give some "standard deviations" and explain them. The main thing is that our prescription almost never goes wrong, that is, as far as I can see, *all* the produced strings will be acceptable, nay, in an overwhelming majority of cases the produced strings will be *the* natural ones:

long$_2$ Polish$_b$ word
big$_2$ beautiful$_h$ red$_f$ Chinese$_b$ silk$_a$ rug
comfortable$_4$ upholstered$_j$ brown$_f$ mahogany$_a$ chair
long$_2$ winding$_j$ asphalt$_a$ road
tall$_2$ dark$_m$ overhanging$_j$ volcanic$_b$ rocks
good$_4$ washable$_l$ white$_f$ cotton$_a$ shirt
small$_2$ frightened$_j$ yellow$_f$ face
fast$_3$ red$_f$ car

huge$_2$ scintillating$_i$ luminous$_h$ blue$_f$ star
large$_2$ striped$_j$ catlike$_c$ Asiatic$_b$ quadruped
deep$_2$ cold$_m$ turbulent$_i$ blue$_f$ waters
small$_2$ strong$_m$ oval$_g$ door
tiny$_2$ rectangular$_g$ yellow$_f$ spots
horrible$_x$ grinning$_i$ toothless$_h$ simian$_b$ mouth
easy$_4$ short$_2$ mathematical$_d$ demonstration
dangerous$_4$ long$_2$ Central-African$_b$ journey

and so on, and so forth.

What happens if we select a mixed bag, that is, some adjectives belonging to the same class, others to different ones? Take *beautiful$_x$, big$_2$, sparkling$_i$, smiling$_i$, blue$_f$* for *eyes*. The result is a "mixed" string:

(1) big beautiful sparkling and smiling blue eyes.

The *and* is obligatory:

big beautiful sparkling smiling blue eyes

sounds unnatural. Similarly:

(2) broad$_2$ and deep$_2$ blue$_f$ river

(3) broken$_j$ and shattered$_j$ human$_b$ bones

are better than

broad deep blue river

broken shattered human bones.

In terms of the symbolism I used above, what happens here can be represented as follows. For (1):

$$\Omega_2 \, (A_2) \, [\Omega_x \, (A_x) \, [\Omega_i \, (A_i \; C \; A_i) \, [\Omega_f \, (A_f) \; N \,]]]$$

for (2) and (3):

$$\Omega_2 \, (A_2 \; C \; A_2) \, [\Omega_f \, (A_f) \; N]$$
$$\Omega_j \, (A_j \; C \; A_j) \, [\Omega_b \, (A_b) \; N]$$

Here I "homogenized" the suffixes to Ω and A. The neat result is this: two or more adjectives belonging to the same class require a connective in prenominal position even if inserted into an otherwise unbroken string. Conversely: truly unbroken strings cannot contain two adjectives of the same class. The connective need not be explicit: comma in writing, and intonation-break in speech suffices. Compare:

long, wide road
long paved road.

3.   In this Section, I shall take up certain irregularities that interfere with the results of Sections 1. and 2. Some of these are general patterns affecting all kinds of adjectives. Others are specific, involving relatively small groups.

Inverted order. — Inversion of the natural order of prenominal adjectives is not absolutely ungrammatical. In that case, however, the adjectives involved have to be taken as belonging not to one but to two nouns, one of them deleted. Take:

He drove out in his new yellow car

versus

He drove out in his yellow new car.

The first adheres to the natural order: new_m, $yellow_f$. Consequently, the sentence means that he drove out in his car which is yellow and which is new. The second sentence cannot be interpreted this way. It means that he drove out in the yellow one of his new cars; i.e.:

yellow new car – the yellow one of the new cars.

Similar interpretation is called for in cases like

She took her Italian$_b$ long$_2$ dress
I mean the yellow$_f$ tall$_2$ building

etc. Incidentally, the same thing holds for comparatives:

This is the shortest good novel I ever read
Use the cleaner small towel

and so forth. So inverted orders can be saved by the following device: given two adjectives A_y and A_z, such as y is higher than z, and given the phrase $A_z\ A_y\ N$, the resolution requires:

$A_z\ A_y\ N$ – the A_z one of the $A_y\ N$'s

Such inverted phrases usually are uttered with a strong emphasis on the first adjective:

yéllow new car.

Moreover, the same strong emphasis is used to indicate selective sense in an orthodox phrase as well:

He drove out in his néw yellow car

is to be taken in the sense of:

the new one of his yellow cars.

Compound-adjectives. — Intonation-pattern is also important to recognize compound-adjectives, like

dárk grèen

gólden yèllow

Prússian blùe

etc. Transformationally they can be recognized by contrasting, say

blue Prussian uniform – uniform wh... is Prussian
                                    uniform wh... is blue

with

Prussian blue uniform – uniform wh... is Prussian blue.

Petrified compounds. — This refers us back to the "unorthodox" transformations affecting A_b's in Chapter VII. There we distinguished

Maltese$_b$ wooden$_a$ cross

from

wooden$_a$ Maltese$_b$ cross

and suggested that in this second case *Maltese* is not tied to *cross* by the standard (α),

cross that is from Malta

but by the special:

cross that is like the one used by the knights of Malta.

Similarly about *Basque hat, Polish notation, Turkish coffee*, etc. Due to the uniqueness of this link, the compound cannot be broken up and any other adjective, regardless of its rank, comes before. Adjectives other than A_b's can form such petrified compounds. Take

English hígh schoòl

tall bádmàn

versus

high English school

?bad tall man

and so on. There is a tendency to pronounce and write these compounds as one unit: hígh-chùrch, bádmàn.

Old, young, little. — This is a troublesome group. The difficulty emerges as soon as we compare:

> big beautiful house
> beautiful little house.

What is the reason for this difference between *big* and *little*? For, notice that

> ? little beautiful house

sounds odd. Similarly *old* and *young* tend to crowd the noun:

> charming little girl
> gray old man

which, obviously, violate the rules of ordering. It seems that these three adjectives tend to form a sort of petrified compound with certain nouns. There are two signs that this may be the case. We can say things like

> Listen, old man, ...
> Little girl, I tell you ...
> I warn you, young lady, ...

but it would be queer to say

> Listen, tall man, ...
> Big girl, I tell you ...
> I warn you, strong lady, ...

Thus these phrases can be used to address people, which is commonly not so with other $A\ N$'s.

The other mark is an interesting one. It involves our derivation of A_3's (VI, 2). We know that the meaning of an A_3N-phrase is a function of an appropriate verb-class determined by the co-occurrence of A_3 and N. Now what happens if we insert another A between the two? Say,

> brave blond man
> good tall woman
> considerate fat girl.

We feel that *blond, tall,* and *fat* are vacuous here. They do not add anything that would modify the aspect under which the subject is called *brave, good* or *considerate.* But now take

brave young man
considerate old lady
good little girl.

These adjectives are by no means vacuous. What transpires here is that while *blond, tall, fat,* etc., just describe the subject, *young, old, little* do more: they specify it as to the things it can be expected to do. So we have in the contrast between

good little girl
? good big girl

a parallel to the contrast of

big beautiful house
beautiful little house.

Emotive adjectives. — In VII, 3, I marked the group of emotive adjectives (horrible, dreadful, etc.) as A_x. This irregular suffix is meant to indicate the irregular place these adjectives can take in a prenominal string. Indeed,

long horrible play
small awful insect
warm delightful room

are as good as

horrible long play
awful small insect
delightful warm room.

There is one difference though. The last three forms are apt to have a strong emphasis on the first adjective, while adjectives in the first three examples carry equal stresses. It seems then that, roughly speaking, A_x's can occur descriptively, in which case they come between A_l's and A_m's, or emotively, with strong stress, in which case they precede anything else.

I also mentioned that certain other adjectives, like *beautiful, lovely,* may carry an emotive load. Hence our hesitation between

Big beautiful tree
Beautiful big tree.

The same holds also of *ugly, dirty* and others:

Little ugly beast
Úgly little beast
Old dirty pig
Dírty old pig
Little yellow rat
Yéllow little rat
Old dirty man
Dírty old man
Young fresh face
Frésh young face.

Thus, unexpectedly, the noted and notorious group of *old*, *young*, and *little* turns up again. Needless to say, in the emphatic cases, *beast*, *rat* and *pig* denote people and not animals. The emphasis with the reversed order and the use of these three adjectives decide in favor of the metaphorical sense. This would not work with other adjectives:

? Úgly small beast
? Yéllow long rat
? Dírty heavy pig.

These five seem to be the main types of irregularity that can interfere with the adjectival order established in Section 2.